THE WEST IN ENGLISH HISTORY

The West
in
English History

Edited by

A. L. ROWSE

HODDER AND STOUGHTON

FIRST PRINTED 1949

Printed in Great Britain by
Northumberland Press Ltd., Gateshead
for Hodder and Stoughton Ltd., London

Foreword

by

GERALD BEADLE

(Controller of the B.B.C.'s West Region)

THE B.B.C.'s West Regional organization speaks most of its time to the four million people who live in the western peninsula of England. But it has many opportunities of speaking to the people of Great Britain, and occasional opportunities of addressing yet more distant audiences. Its task is to reflect the life, achievements and history of the West Country. There are, of course, differences of opinion as to where the West Country begins, but all are agreed that it ends at the Bishop Rock, far out in the Atlantic Ocean. It is a region of great diversity, and its unity is a product of its diversity. It bears the marks of Mediterranean, Celtic, Roman, West Saxon and Norman influences. They are apparent in its earthworks, mines, castles and cathedrals, in its names, traditions and customs, its counties, boroughs and villages. It was the birthplace of metalliferous mining and in more recent times of the factory system.

5

It has played a leading part in England's maritime history. Indeed it played a leading part in England's very emergence as a united nation, and in all that has arisen from that momentous happening during the last thousand years.

It is therefore not surprising that we should presume to interpret England's story in a West Country setting. Nor is it surprising that a West Saxon producer from Gloucestershire (Gilbert Phelps) should collaborate with a Celtic historian from Cornwall (A. L. Rowse) in planning the project.

I myself derived enormous pleasure and profit from listening to the talks which are reproduced in this volume, and there is strong evidence to suggest that about a hundred thousand other West Countrymen did so too. This subsequent publication in print is not a B.B.C. enterprise. All the credit for it goes to the publishers and to the speakers, who own the copyright in their respective contributions. For myself I welcome the book very warmly, because I know it throws fresh light on the history of our nation in a setting small and intimate enough to grip the imagination. I welcome it too because it supplies what radio always fails to supply—permanence. These talks were so good that they deserve permanence.

Contents

The West in English History

Note

These essays, originally broadcast, seek to open up and suggest themes for further exploration, rather than to exhaust them. We owe them to the inspiration of Gilbert Phelps, of the B.B.C. Western Regional, to whose fertility in ideas the West is indebted for so many good series and talks. I should like to pay tribute to his wide sympathies of mind, his fresh responsiveness, his sense of the richness and diversity of English life in its roots in the various regions.

A.L.R.

I

Introductory
by
A. L. ROWSE

This series offers you something new, I think, in the way of talks. The idea of it is to show you something of the part the West has played in English life, and in return the effect that some of the great events in the nation's history have had upon us down here in the West.

It fits in with—indeed it expresses—what I think is the most interesting development in our way of seeing and writing history nowadays: I mean the way of looking not just at the top surface of events, but trying to grasp the life of society as a whole through all its layers, economic and political, social and cultural. Naturally that makes history very difficult to write—to carry it all along with one. And the best way of cutting the cake is to take a good slice downwards, cutting off some particular well-defined region in which we may sample the characteristics of the whole. Of course it can, and should be, done for any region; but what more fascinating than the one that lies on our own doorsteps—all round us—the West?

That links up with the way of seeing and writing history that particularly interests friends of mine, and which I think the most promising new line of development in historical studies: the synthesis of local and national history, bringing together the things that lie beneath our own eyes—the landscape, buildings of all kinds, people—and using our imagination to see and understand through them the life of the whole country and people to which we belong.

As I write these words, I look out across the Cornish fields and winter-green bay, to the entrance to Fowey harbour. And I think of all the memories of Fowey: the tit-for-tat raids across the Channel to the Norman and Breton seaports, ending up with the burning of the town and the gallant defence of Place House in 1457 by the Mrs. Treffry of the day. Or I think of the landing of Philip of Spain's treasures there, and how they stowed it away—that clever dodge of Elizabeth's by which his troops in the Netherlands went unpaid and mutinied, and the independence of the Low Countries was saved. I almost fancy I can see the Parliamentarian troops camping out there along the Gribbin where they were surrounded in the Civil War. Or I remember the Parliamentarian soldier who deposed, when it was all over and the King was on trial for his life, that on a day in 1644 he had seen Charles

Stuart riding in front of his troops on St. Austell Downs —just in front of my house. Everybody knows Charles I's majestic letter of thanks for the loyalty of his county of Cornwall, written after the victorious campaign of 1644.—perhaps by that great Wiltshireman, Edward Hyde: you can still see that letter hanging up in our churches.

Or if I could see outside the walls of the studio here in Bristol where I am speaking, my eyes would rest on the richest collection of evidences of the most famous and storied town in the West. (The fact that there has been so much destruction here by the bloody barbarians —of both kinds—makes it all the more important to treasure what is left.) I think of all those early Bristol merchants with their interests in the medieval wine trade to Bordeaux and in fishing right up to Iceland: I think of the great merchant, William Cannynges, sleeping there to-night in his tomb in the splendid church he built—St. Mary Redcliffe—monument to his wealth, his taste and his piety; and there is the shadow of the tragic young poet of genius, Chatterton, haunting the room above the porch. It was those Bristol merchants who set on foot the first voyages to find out the New World across the Atlantic; it was from here that the Cabots set out to discover Newfoundland.

There is an endless fascination and pleasure in looking upon the places we inhabit and exploring the richness of their associations—I don't think of them as *past*. History isn't something that is dead and done with; it is something that is alive and all round us, in our blood and bones, in our memories, in our head—if we have any head—in the things we see before our eyes. To know about these things gives us more life, enriches the sense of life immeasurably, inexhaustibly —whereas the trouble with so many people is that they are so bored they don't know what to do with themselves. It is all the more important to have our eyes open to the riches of this kind, when it is almost all we have got left to us, I sometimes think. And all the more essential to appreciate the character, the idiosyncrasy, the diversity and richness of the regions of England in a time when the great danger is the indignity, the shamelessness, the vulgar and cheap insipidity of a Hollywood civilization, with the ruin of towns that had both integration and integrity, the spawning of suburbia and industrial slumdom across the gentlest and loveliest countryside of the world.

All sensitive minds respond to these deeper layers of experience that are about us and have made us.

> *Time and the ocean and some fostering star*
> *In high cabal have made us what we are.*

This is the best short summing-up of the history of England, written by a poet.

I remember John Masefield telling me that when Thomas Hardy was building his house, Max Gate, just outside Dorchester, he wasn't happy about it because it was new and raw and without history. Then they found that the ground was partly on a Roman cemetery, and brooches and fibulae and all sorts of things came up when they were excavating—then it was all right, and Hardy was contented. You will find traces of this in one or two of Hardy's poems; and again in the charming little museum at Dorchester. Lawrence of Arabia found the same thing in talking to Hardy—you remember that wonderful letter describing the experience?—how the war to him was the great Napoleonic War and his mind full of its memories: he saw the events of to-day in their true perspective, as from a serene height. No English novelist—save Sir Walter and he was a Scot—was more filled with the sense of history, the sense of the continuity and pathos of life under the sentence of time, than Hardy: it is what gives him his philosophical greatness and makes him perhaps the greatest of all English novelists. The West has undying reason to be proud of him.

Or take the sense of the past of England that gave a second breath of inspiration to a great writer who was educated in the West, though he did not write about it except for his book *Stalky and Co.* This sense runs through many of Kipling's books and poems, such a book as *Puck of Pook's Hill*:

See you the dimpled track that runs,
All hollow through the wheat?
O that was where they hauled the guns
That smote King Philip's fleet.

See you our little mill that clacks,
So busy by the brook?
She has ground her corn and paid her tax
Ever since Doomsday Book.

The greatest and most enduring of English writers, Shakespeare, had a fine historical sense, and his interest was obviously keenly engaged by history; while the next greatest of our poets, Milton, was a practising historian. (You may not know that he wrote not only a history of Britain, but a history of Russia.) I take it that the case is proved. These great writers spring from our soil and are just as much a part of what we inherit from the past as churches and buildings, the memories of the landscape.

A most sensitive mind among contemporary historians, F. M. Powicke, has written thus: "Shepherds have kept their sheep in all ages: why am I stirred so deeply because I can trace the very sheep-walks of the monks of Furness? Why is there a remote, yet strangely familiar, music about the names of places—Beverley, Gainsborough, Thrapston, Tewkesbury—a music in which it is impossible to distinguish the call of authentic English speech from the echoes of a hundred insistent associations? . . . It is the sense of the past that comes to us from the Middle Ages as it came to the young American in Henry James's story, as he wandered about his eighteenth-century house in London —'the sense of a conscious past, recognizing no less

than recognizable'. The place was a museum, 'but a
museum of held reverberations'."

Powicke, you see, is a North Countryman—though
he comes as far west as Tewkesbury for his reverberations, those remembered echoes. But indeed we need
feel no inferiority to the North—splendid as that is—
with our own more intimate treasures. Glastonbury,
Cerne Abbas, Brympton D'Evercy, Montacute, Buckland Monachorum, St. Michael's Mount—these places
have no less "held reverberations" for us—like the
sound of church bells at Christmas or Epiphany coming across moorland or hillside or the western sea.

But not only what places with their memories, what
subjects we have to offer you. We have got together a
team of the best authorities to deal with their respective
subjects from the Romans right up to the end of the
Victorian Age. For the Victorian Age, for example,
who better than the poet who has retrieved Victorian
architecture for us, opened our eyes to its beauties,
written a new chapter—or at least a paragraph—in the
history of taste: John Betjeman? For the Romans in
the West we have got you a leading Roman historian
from Cambridge. (The eastern counties, alas, have not
got a Regional of their own; but I am a strong believer
in bringing out the character and local inflections of
our regions, exploring and understanding them, all the
more when there is so much danger of a dull level of
sameness, a uniform characterlessness in our time.)

I suppose it is true to say that never has the West

more decisively affected the history of England than in the career of Alfred of Wessex: but for him England would have been conquered by the Danes; through him England remained English. We shall hear about him from a high Wessex authority, G. M. Young.

The next most decisive contributions of the West to English history have been in relation to the sea—which you will hear about from Dr. Williamson and Professor Macinnes.

Three talks deal with the historic industries of the West: Mr. Ramsay with the famous old cloth-making industry, once foremost in the land; Mr. Beatty with trade and transport; Mr. Harris with Cornwall's part in the Industrial Revolution. The actual making of the landscape and the way the story of West Country people is printed on its face—a fascinating topic—is treated by Mr. Hoskins. We are not able to deal in detail with prehistory, which is rather a separate subject, but Mr. Hoskins tells us something of how the prehistoric shows through the landscape of to-day—the small Celtic fields that can be seen from the air lying underneath our modern ones, such places as Maiden Castle, Avebury, Stonehenge. Geoffrey Grigson describes the land as Cobbett saw it on the threshhold of the nineteenth century. Something of the cultural side of life in the West is given us by Mr. Summerson in his talk on eighteenth-century Bath and by Mr. Betjeman.

So much for most of the topics: they cannot possibly

cover all the ground: they are chosen to give you an idea of its extent.

But, after all, there is no region that has exerted such a pull on the imagination, on mind and heart, as the West does; and that you can see in the works of painters, poets and musicians no less than in novelists and historians. It happens that a great many people have written well about the West: either they belonged to it or were struck by it and loved it. Let me suggest when winter comes, and lights are lit, curtains drawn in little houses on hillsides, in the valleys, along the coast at home, that you get out the books and follow up these talks, explore the themes we can only touch on. There you will find for yourselves endless entertainment, profit and amusement.

II

The Romans in the South-West

by

M. P. CHARLESWORTH

To-night we are to think about the South-West in Roman times and under Roman occupation; perhaps at the outset we ought to ask ourselves why it was that the Romans ever occupied our island at all. We are so accustomed to the fact of a Roman occupation which lasted for nearly four hundred years, that we are apt to regard it almost as a law of nature. Julius Caesar merely raided us. It was a rather unwarlike emperor, Claudius, who began the permanent occupation: he wanted a striking success to mark the opening years of his rule, and so sent Roman commanders and four Roman legions to this island in the year 43.

His successor, the emperor Nero, for a time actually contemplated abandoning it; but although it was probably a hundred years before our province began properly to pay its way, it eventually proved so useful and profitable because of its mineral wealth, and of its agricultural riches, and (possibly) as a military training-ground, that Rome went on occupying it till well after the year 400. When our South-West comes into the light of recorded history—and in the term South-West I am going to include not only Cornwall, Devon and Somerset, but the adjacent parts on north and east of Gloucestershire and Dorsetshire as well—most of the region was occupied by a tribe called the Dumnonii (from their name, by the way, the later word Devon ultimately derives). What did the Romans do with this Dumnonian part of our country?

To answer that question I am going to divide our territory into three regions:

1. The first region includes the country on both sides of the lower Severn; here lay the mineral resources, the iron of the Forest of Dean, and the lead of the Mendips; and we may remark that the mines of the Mendips were being worked by the Romans within six years of the conquest, that is by A.D. 49. In the early stages slave or convict labour must have been employed, and this would be supervised by military guards, detachments sent over from the great legionary centre of Caerleon (near Newport, Mon.). For though the Second Legion, the one that originally over-ran the South-West, was for a time encamped near Gloucester, it had moved by A.D. 75 to Caerleon, to stay there for the next two hundred years. Apart from the mineral wealth, there was the spa (and healing waters) of Bath. Here the visitor can still see the great cold plunge-bath, lead-lined, with

22

the steps that led down into it; still form some notion
of the great complex of buildings that the site included,
even though they are but magnificent remains. Most
impressive of all, perhaps, he can still gaze on the fierce
Gorgon-head that decorated the centre of the shield on
the pediment of the temple of Sulis Minerva, the god-
dess of the spa; here the artist has produced no formal
"classical" mask, but a glaring and ferocious male head
with moustache and beard, whose locks intertangle
with the snaky hair in a terrifying rhythm—one of the
finest monuments of Romano-Celtic sculpture. Hither,
as inscriptions reveal, all sorts of people congregated "to
take the waters".

One further place, farther up the Severn, Lydney,
seems also to have been a spa and a place of pilgrimage.
You will note there was no Roman equivalent of Bristol,
and ask yourselves why.

2. The second region includes the farming estates
(*villae*, the Romans called them) of southern Gloucester,
western Dorset and eastern Somerset. The prosperity
of this region endured for at least two centuries (say
from 130 to 330). Its extreme western boundary is the
city of Exeter, where the recent excavations of Lady
Fox have revealed the earliness of the Roman occupation. For the Romans realized that this site was the
key to the West, as the Normans showed by building a
castle there, and as the siege of Exeter in our Civil War
also demonstrated. We know little about the tribal
history of the Dumnonii, but we do know that Exeter

was their capital city, and we know also that at some period they contributed to the repair of the great Roman Wall that spans north England, either by sending native labourers or by money levies; an inscribed stone found not far from Thirlwall castle on the line of the Wall records the name of the Dumnonii as responsible for a section.

3. The third region is what we might call provisionally the unoccupied zone; I do not believe that the Romans ever permanently occupied the whole tract of country west of Exeter. They mostly left it to itself; just as in Wales they left the Lleyn peninsula alone and as in Scotland they left Galloway alone. Still, there was, after all, the tin of Cornwall; for some sixty or seventy years, say from 70-140, there seems to have existed a temporary settlement near Tregear, a couple of miles from Bodmin. But there were no through roads, and communication must have been by sea; although it looks as though some Dumnonian nobleman built for himself a Roman-style house at Magor near Camborne (in Illogan parish), Roman influence was slight.

Later on, however, when Spanish tin supplies failed in the late third century, Cornish tin came into its own, and some short stretches of road must have been built under Roman orders; the proof of that is four late Roman milestones found in western Cornwall.

Probably the greatest prosperity was enjoyed by the farming estates, with their associated rural industries, in the *villa* region; in Somerset alone there were about

sixty such *villae*, and one of the most sensational finds
of recent years is that of a villa at Low Ham (near
Bridgwater), where an early timber farm-house had been
rebuilt in grander style towards the end of the third
century, and a fine bath-house added, with a most
remarkable mosaic representing scenes from Vergil's
Aeneid. This find demonstrates that even in the fourth
century life was going sufficiently well for the owner
to rebuild expensively, and that he was a man of considerable wealth and culture; in fact these villa-owners
probably included men of education and of taste, and
were by no means a mere squirearchy. Perhaps the
most noteworthy example of such a villa is to be found,
not in Somerset, but still in our South-West, at Ched-
worth in Gloucestershire, some half-dozen miles north
of Cirencester. Here, on higher ground that slopes
pleasantly down a little valley towards the east, have
been excavated the foundations of an extensive farming estate: a large outer court comprised barns and
storehouses, with living quarters for the workmen, slave
or free; within a second and smaller court lay the house
of the owner, with a fine dining-room, baths and garden,
with quarters, too, for domestic servants, while the
northern wing housed a forge and fulling establishment.

But before the middle of the fourth century this
prosperous region was beginning to suffer from the raids
of Irish pirates, and a sign of that still remains in the
two Roman signal-stations which were identified by Mr.
Bushe Fox on the headland at Martinhoe and at Old

Burrow, not far from Lynton. These could give early warning of the approach of hostile craft, and the country could be put on the alert. What one would like to know is to what points were these signals to be flashed; to Exeter? or to the *villa* region of eastern Somerset? or across the Bristol Channel to the garrison at Caerleon? And where were the other signal-stations, for others there must have been? Up to the present moment we simply do not know.

However, after nearly four centuries, the Roman occupation ended; the legions had to be withdrawn to meet threats nearer the centre of the Empire, and even before they left continual and savage raids from Irish and from Saxon pirates had caused havoc in the coastal regions, and lowered the standard of living of the inhabitants. But the occupation was no mere episode in our history—for consider some of the things that remained. First and most obvious the magnificent road-system, which linked and unified the country, and upon which a great deal of our modern road-system is still based. Secondly, the sites of cities and towns; Exeter, Dorchester, Bath, Gloucester and Cirencester are still places of importance, and they owe their foundation to Rome. And thirdly, Rome had introduced in the fourth century a religion, Christianity. Though material remains are scanty—a small church at Caerwent, an inscription denoting the presence of a Christian community at Cirencester—yet thanks to the evangelizing energy of a Roman-British citizen, St.

Patrick, who converted Ireland, that country, in the dark days after the Roman withdrawal, was able to reinforce Christianity in some parts and introduce it in others. From the Celtic West, whence once had come the raiders, now came missionaries and monks; monks who settled at Glastonbury, or missionaries such as St. Samson; that holy man, journeying through Cornwall, was shocked to find some of the country people worshipping "an abominable image", and so took appropriate action.

Thus to some extent the Romans had already laid down the pattern of later life in this country—the main lines of communication, the sites of towns and cities—and I think they had also introduced many of the trees, fruit-trees and flowers which now adorn our countryside and our gardens.

But whereas they had exploited the rich farming lands of Somerset, and exploited our mineral resources, observe that Cornwall had been left pretty well alone and practically isolated from the life of Roman Britain, and so could develop upon its own lines. When Angles and Saxons came here, and fought over these lands for the next four centuries, their campaigns were often based upon those roads that the Romans had bequeathed to them, the limit of their penetration for centuries was Exeter, and their character and civilization was eventually moulded by that very religion which the Romans had introduced.

III

Alfred of Wessex

by

G. M. YOUNG

PERHAPS you have read—and no one who has read it will ever forget—a passage in the *Stones of Venice* where Ruskin describes the landscape of Europe as a stork or a swallow might see it in its flight, from Syria or Greece, Italy or Spain, laid like pieces of gold pavement in deep sea blue; then the belt of forest green, with grey swirls of rain clouds and mighty brooks: and so, still north, till even the forests fail and the wall of ice set its teeth against us out of the polar twilight.

Now all that vast region was the roving ground of the Norsemen. Some of them pushed east into the Russian plains, and so down the Russian rivers to the Black Sea and Constantinople, where they might meet kinsfolk who had come the other way through the Straits of Gibraltar. Some settled in the Orkneys, some in Iceland: some still more adventurous made their way to Greenland, some sighted the coast of America.

Every year, when spring came, fleets of open-decked war boats left the fjords of Norway or the creeks of Denmark to plunder, or if they liked the land, to settle. And England was a very tempting prey. Those broad, slow rivers of the eastern side, the Ouse, the Trent, the Thames, gave access to the heart of the country and then—draw up your galleys, build a rampart or a stockade about them, round up all the horses you can lay hands on, and then off and away to burn and plunder. And the odds were heavy on the invaders. On the one side, men trained to act together, knowing that they must win or perish: and on the other, farming folk hurriedly summoned from the harvest or the plough. They could fight from morning to evening. But when evening came they preferred to walk home and leave the heathen men in possession of their fields. If you can imagine the Home Guard eight years ago, with no backing of regular troops, trying to deal with airborne descents here, there and everywhere all at once, you will have some idea of what the Danish onslaught meant. "This year," says the Chronicle, "there were nine pitched battles south of Thames besides encounters with the King and his officers which no one reckoned." That was the year King Alfred came to the throne.

What sort of man was he? So far, all we hear of him is that he was born at Wantage in Berkshire, and was evidently the flower of the royal flock, a handsome, attractive boy, fond of hunting and spouting poetry: not so fond of learning his lessons but quick at them when he did. And he had had an adventure which I suppose had never befallen a young English prince before. He had crossed the Alps. He had been twice to Rome, to be hallowed by the Pope, to be confirmed, that is, and invested with the robes of a Roman Consul. So when, years later, he came to translate the Roman history for the instruction of his people, he was writing of things and places he had seen. We know, too, that as a young man he was afflicted with a mysterious illness, and that he spent the greater part of his life in pain. And that is all—the rest we must divine from what he did. And what was that?

First of all he had to win a breathing space for the kingdom of Wessex. The rest of England was to all intents and purposes lost. But those nine pitched battles showed the invaders that Wessex, though small, was uncommonly tough, and so long as Wessex and its King stood fast there was hope that Christianity would not be ultimately submerged by the heathen men. And the heathen men knew it. So, learning that the King was keeping Christmas at Chippenham in Wiltshire, they pounced. They were in the heart of the kingdom: all they had to do was to wait till the spring came and the rest of the kingdom would tumble into their hands: and England would be a base for a grand attack on France.

Meanwhile where was the King? With a handful of guards, by forest and marsh, he had made his way into Somerset. His headquarters were that little knoll, then an island in the waste of Sedgmoor, Athelney. From there when early summer came the orders went out, "In the seventh week after Easter, Somerset, Wiltshire and Hampshire this side of Southampton water are to be with me at Egbert's Stone."

If the Danes could pounce, so could the King. They marched south to meet him, and they did meet him, at Edington in Wiltshire. There the great battle was fought, and this time the Danes owned themselves fairly beaten. Those that were left promised to quit the kingdom: their leader agreed to be baptized—that was at Aller, near Athelney—the campaign ended with a christening feast and presents all round at Wedmore, and, except for a few snatching raids along the south coast, no Dane entered the kingdom again. There was plenty of fighting still, but all of it outside our borders. Wessex had been saved.

But how to keep it safe from a fresh attack? The mischief lay in the mobility of the invaders, who could come and go while the local levies were being collected to deal with them. Now there still exists a document which, though badly copied, contains, I think, the King's own answer to this problem—a loop of fortified towns beginning in Sussex, running west to Exeter, then leaping across to the Bristol Channel and returning eastward. And this girdle of strongholds was locked, as it were, by London, which was already one of the greatest ports of the northern world. London, of course, was too far off to be included in the West-Saxon kingdom, so it was handed over for safe keeping to the Midlanders and their regent, who had married Alfred's daughter. For a long while it had seemed doubtful where the future capital of England would be. Will it be Wilton, the ancestral home of the royal house? Or Winchester, the mother church of the kingdom? Or Exeter, or that other great port, Bristol? Alfred made it certain that it would be London. And then, says the chronicler, all England, except those who were under Danish thraldom, "acknowledged him as King".

He was now a man of thirty-eight, and there were seven years of peace in front of him before the Danish storm broke again. We must not forget those two visits to Rome and what they meant to a boy who had never seen anything grander than the narrow streets, the timber houses, and the small cathedral at Winchester. Or perhaps the Roman ruins of Bath. Besides which Alfred came of a family which had links with the Continent: his grandfather had spent thirteen years in France, his father had taken a French princess for his second wife, and to any thoughtful man it must have been plain that these Danish inroads threatened not England alone, or France alone, but the whole of the Christian West. But England under these terrible ravages was losing her place in western civilization altogether. And civilization meant Latin. Whether it was history or philosophy or plain morality, Latin was the key to the best that had been thought and written in the world. It was the language of the Church

C

—and even among the clergy in England how many priests, how many monks were left who could spell their way through a service book? Of course for laymen, for the King's officers and commanders in the field, Latin was not necessary. Then they should have the substance of the great Latin books in their own native tongue. So first the King must master the language himself, and to this end he gathered a little group of scholars about him, an Englishman, a German, a Welshman, to help him with his Latin. As they explained it, so he turned it into his own English. On the Feast of St. Martin, November 11th, when he was in his fortieth year, he made the first entry in the handbook he always carried about with him—verses from the Bible, sayings of the Christian fathers, notes about his own family history, or the tale of St. Aldhelm, Abbot of Malmesbury and Bishop of Sherborne who would take his stand, like a minstrel, on the bridge and gather a congregation by singing stories of old times. And Aldhelm's verses, the King said, were the best he knew.

Seven years of peace, and then three years of war again, with pestilence and cattle plague, but the kingdom stood and the work went on. Now that the old kingdoms, Kent, Wessex and Mercia were coming together in one realm, they needed a common book of law—simple rules for the guidance of the local courts in doing justice or fixing a penalty. Suppose two men are felling a tree and it falls and kills one of them, what

34

does the law say? Answer: the tree or its value goes to the dead man's family as compensation. And we have a delightful glimpse of the King at Wardour in Wiltshire washing his hands in the inner room while his councillors lay a case before him. But war or peace, however busy the King may be, the work of turning Latin books into English goes on. First comes a book for the parish priests, the *Pastoral Care* of the great Pope Gregory who sent Augustine to England. Then, for laymen rather, the *History of the World* by the Spaniard Orosius, in which the King has inserted much that interested him and his people about the geography of the northern parts from which the invaders came. And in the last few years of peace he set himself his hardest task, to turn into English the last great book of antiquity, the *Consolation of Philosophy* by Boethius. Morality, history, philosophy, the King had rounded the circle, and looking back on his work he said he felt like a man who had gone into a forest, and on every tree he saw something that would be useful to him. It was only a light load, after all, that he had brought home. But others would come after him with wagons, and fetch timber and build houses, where they might live winter and summer happily and in peace. "As I have never done," said the King.

IV

The Norman Conquest in the West

by

PROFESSOR DAVID DOUGLAS

Have you ever thought how many of the episodes in the familiar story of the Norman Conquest were of special concern to the West Country, and have you ever considered why it was that our region should have played such an important part in that great crisis of English history? Winchester was the first great city whose submission was demanded by the Conqueror, and at Winchester four years later he was to be crowned afresh. In 1068 one of the most important episodes of the Conquest took place outside the walls of Exeter, and late in the reign it was at Salisbury that the King held a great assembly to secure the fidelity of his greater subjects. No part of England was more affected than ours by the Norman Conquest, and I want this evening to ask why this was so.

Perhaps in one sense it was inevitable. The battle of Hastings may or may not have been a national disaster, but it was certainly a special defeat for Wessex. Harold the commander who there fought and died had been for thirteen years Earl of Wessex, and only for nine months doubtfully King of England, and much of his career had been spent in extending the power of Wessex over the other English provinces. After the first defeat, then, it was inevitable that resistance should form in the West, and it was equally natural that the new King would specially wish to secure Exeter, the south-western capital. So it was for this reason that the Conqueror in January 1068 marched for the first time into the West. Some of the chief men in the city offered to give it up, but their fellow citizens refused, and when William arrived outside its walls he found the gates closed against him. In fact he had to besiege Exeter for eighteen days, and finally he only entered it on conditions. He was probably glad of the compromise. The North of England was already restive; there was a threat of an invasion from Scandinavia, and the south-western capital was essential to his defence. At all events Exeter was not punished for its resistance, and William actually set up a kind of military police to prevent his soldiers from plundering the citizens.

You can look up for yourselves a graphic account of this campaign by an early chronicler, so now I only want to make three short comments upon it. Firstly, the opponents of William in the West received little support from other parts of England. Secondly, the

Conqueror had English soldiers in his own army. And thirdly, after the submission of Exeter the new King never again had to encounter serious opposition in the West Country. These facts are significant. They suggest, I think, that the opposition to William was provincial rather than local, and that the new King from the start had his own party in England. Indeed, when later in the same year the sons of Harold landed at Avonmouth it was the men of Bristol who repulsed them. The citizens evidently thought that in the circumstances their welfare could best be safeguarded by a strong king from overseas. And who shall say that they were wrong?

It is for these reasons that almost immediately after the submission of Exeter a number of new figures began to appear in the West Country, for the first and most important result of the Norman Conquest was the establishment of a new landed aristocracy. The greater Saxon families passed very rapidly out of the picture, and twenty years after the submission of Exeter there were hardly any of them left. Their place was taken by a new nobility. Almost the whole of Cornwall, for instance, passed into the hands of the King's half-brother, Robert, Count of Mortain. At Exeter there was established as sheriff Baldwin of Meules, the son of Count Gilbert of Brionne, and Bristol was placed in charge of another Norman noble, Geoffrey of Mowbray who was also Bishop of Coutances. The establishment of these men and of other similar families was, in fact, the most revolutionary consequence of the Norman Conquest. They are worth watching. For much of the history of the West Country for the next hundred years will be essentially a record of their acts.

One of the most striking symbols of their authority were those motte and bailey castles which are characteristic of the Norman period. At Winchester the King himself built a castle just outside the walls, and a still more famous castle was erected at Exeter. It is perhaps surprising that this Exeter castle is not mentioned in Domesday Book, but we know from other sources that William himself ordered it to be built, and although it is very possible that it was built on a site which had previously been fortified, there is no reason to doubt that the familiar Rougemont castle is essentially a Norman creation.

This Norman aristocracy which thus came into the West was not only powerful, it was also small and compact. It was knit together by intermarriage and joined by common interests to the King. These men had almost as much to lose by feudal rebellion as had the King himself, and no student of West Country history in this period can be happy in the doctrine that the dominant theme of Anglo-Norman history was a constant struggle between Crown and Baronage. Rather it was the successful operation of a new system of government by an exceedingly able group of men with the King at their head. These men and others like them held their lands in return for providing trained and equipped soldiers to fight in the royal army, and it was their duty to supply counsel to the King and to support his acts. In return the King left most of the details of local government in their hands. The results of their rule can indeed nowhere be better seen than in the place-names of Devon. Churston *Ferrers*, Bovey *Tracey*, Berry *Pomeroy*, Weston *Peveril* (to name no others) indicate unmistakably how firmly the great feudal families of Norman England became rooted in the West Country soil.

And it was not only secular government which they transformed. A characteristic feature of the Norman Conquest in the West was the establishment by prelates of foreign birth of a pattern of ecclesiastical administration that has survived with little modification till to-day. Before the coming of Duke William, Bishop Leofric of Crediton had moved his see to Exeter, and in 1078 the combined sees of Sherborne and Ramsbury were transferred to Salisbury. Moreover, the men who here became prelated were usually men of mark. Thurstan, Abbot of Glastonbury, who caused a scandal by using soldiers to chastise his monks, was a notorious but also an exceptional figure. At Winchester Bishop Walkelin was famed as an organizer, and at Salisbury Osmund was later venerated as a saint. But for the most part these Norman prelates were hard, practical men, and they were great builders. The beloved outline of Exeter cathedral with its twin towers did not, it is true, take its familiar shape until the time of

Henry I, but it was the outcome of Norman principles of building, and at Winchester Bishop Walkelin rebuilt the old minster, where his transepts remain to this day virtually untouched. No lover of the West Country can ignore those massive, rounded arches which the Normans bequeathed as an inheritance to so many of its parish churches.

And what of the ordinary folk? What of the ordinary citizens of Winchester and Exeter, the burgesses of Bristol and Bridport, the inhabitants of the scattered villages of Somerset and Devon? Paradoxically, I do not think that these were at first—at least—very generally affected by the Norman Conquest. The misfortunes of the West in the campaigns of 1066-1070 have, I think, been exaggerated, and there seems to have been little wanton destruction. Winchester and Exeter received favourable terms from the Conqueror, and Bristol seems to have been ready to accept his rule. Soon, too, a revival of trade was to benefit the towns of England. As for the peasantry, their condition depended very largely upon village customs which varied from place to place, and if we may trust the evidence of Domesday Book, these do not seem to have been much modified by the Conquest. Peasant life remained servile and hard, but not worse, I think, in 1100 than it had been in 1050.

The chief loss to the West Country from the Norman Conquest was, I think, that vernacular culture which had been its especial glory, and which was now to dwindle and die. In the transmission of that ancient Saxon culture, however, a notable part was to be played by Norman Exeter. After the death of Bishop Leofric of Exeter in 1072, the manuscripts which he had brought with him from Crediton passed into the charge of his successor. His name was Osbern, and he belonged to the inner circle of the Norman nobility. But he had come to England in the reign of Edward the Confessor, and we are expressly told that he had learnt to respect the customs of Englishmen. We may, therefore, suspect that it was partly owing to his custodianship that Exeter is to-day particularly rich in early manuscripts, and that in particular she possesses that most notable Anglo-Saxon text—the Exeter book of Old English verse. There is something to my mind not a little significant that it was a Norman prelate closely related to the Conqueror who preserved for posterity one of the four most important surviving collections of Anglo-Saxon poetry.

The most enduring benefit which the Normans conferred upon Wessex was to make her feel more strictly that she was a part of England. These Norman magnates controlling their scattered estates upon a uniform feudal plan, this royal administration operating over the whole of the land, were creating a new notion of English political unity. This, however, the people of the time could hardly have foreseen. What they were conscious of was the spreading benefit of a strong rule. Over all the achievement of the Normans in the West

towers the figure of the Conqueror himself—perhaps
the greatest king ever to occupy the English throne.
He was a man to fear rather than to love, but he was
no tyrant nor was he regarded as one. Hampshire saw
him at his worst, but though the making of the New
Forest was a crime, it must be remembered that royal
forests jealously preserved had been a feature of English life before he came, and in general the personal
impress of the Conqueror on Wessex was both bene-
ficial and lasting. The very fact that the great redis-
tribution of land was here effected without anarchy is
a tribute to his overmastering administration. He
created a system of government which under his direction could preserve order, and by doing this he discharged the most difficult and the most important duty
of a medieval king. For that reason ordinary folk, like
you and me, who feared his anger, were ready to support him because of the "good peace" which he maintained. And it was an Englishman who wrote at his
death: "This was a very wise man and very powerful,
and more to be honoured than were any of his pre-
decessors as Kings of England."

V

The Monasteries of the West

by

PROFESSOR R. F. TREHARNE

Cıvilization in Western England stands on monastic foundations. When Roman life in Britain slowly foundered in a rising tide of barbaric, heathen ignorance, the monks alone laboured to stem the flood. Wellborn youths of Roman and Christian family tradition answered the brutish challenge of those pagan times. Vowing themselves to the missionary life, they became disciples of famous abbots, like St. Martin of Tours, in the great monasteries of Gaul and Italy. Having mastered the doctrines of their faith and the rules of monastic life, they returned home and, in the secure South-West, sheltered still from the menacing Saxon sword, they taught by precept and example the faith they had learned. Wales and Ireland, newly converted, soon sent powerful reinforcements to their ranks. It was the Age of Saints, whose names often adorn no calendar, but were so well remembered by those for whom they laboured that they still appear, scattered throughout the western shires, St. Briavels, St. Budeaux, St. Decumans, St. Mawes, and dozens more like them. Their visionary asceticism, their humble devotion to the Gospel, brought them disciples everywhere. They lifted men's lives above sordid materialism and savage greed, and they built in the West the foundations of a Christian civilization.

Their monasteries, simple churches surrounded by wattle huts, proclaimed everywhere a better way of life. Glastonbury, hallowed by ancient legends both true and imaginary, was the most famous shrine in Britain, venerated long before ever the Saxons reached the ridge of the Mendips above its marshy vale. When at length they forced the forest barrier which had shielded the West so long, the invaders, too, had become Christian, ready to receive the precious heritage of faith and culture from their conquered British subjects in the rising kingdom of Wessex. That there was a heritage to transmit was due wholly to those Celtic monks who, unsupported by mighty popes or powerful kings, had established Christian civilization out of chaotic savagery.

Celtic fervour of faith and delight in learning now blended with Saxon ardour, producing miraculous fruit in the first generation. By A.D. 700, Wessex, a beacon of religion and learning, was pouring light across England into the dark forests of pagan Germany. English monks and scholars surpassed their Celtic teachers in zeal for Christianity and love of classical learning. St. Aldhelm, the first learned Englishman, studied under the Irish monk and scholar St. Maildubh, whose name Malmesbury perpetuates, and then under the Canterbury scholars, Archbishop Theodore of Tarsus and Hadrian the African. Aldhelm made Malmesbury the greatest missionary centre and school in Wessex. Leading thousands to the Christian way of life, he planted Christianity in Wessex on secure foundations, and became the best-loved bishop and foremost scholar of his day. A yet greater Saxon monk, St. Boniface of Crediton, was murdered by Frisian pagans in 755, but not until he had so firmly established Christianity in the Rhineland and Germany that nothing could shake it for nearly twelve centuries.

In Wessex the flame lit by the monks burned so brightly that even the Danish invasions could not wholly extinguish it. West Saxon monks were foremost in aiding Alfred and his descendants in the tremendous task of rebuilding England. Greatest of all was St. Dunstan, Abbot of Glastonbury, Bishop of Worcester and London, Archbishop of Canterbury, of whom legend tells that when the Devil tempted him in the guise of a glamour-girl, the Saint, undeceived by this unlikely disguise, seized a pair of tongs and tweaked the infernal nose. Actually, Dunstan was one of the great makers of England. Since the King was a mere boy, and the kingdom rent by faction, Dunstan took control of England. He so guided King, clergy and nobles, that his thirty years' government is rightly called the Golden Age of Anglo-Saxon England. He and his great friends, St. Ethelwold of Winchester and St. Oswald of Worcester, purified and reorganized the Church, restored the monasteries and revived the glory of English learning. Although death removed the powerful impulse of his guidance in 988, his work endured so well that eighty years later, the Norman Conquest found the Church in England stronger, purer and more cultured than in almost any other land.

Meanwhile the life and work of the monk had changed fundamentally. Christianity had conquered Europe, and the Anglo-Celtic missionary monk was no longer required. The Roman rule of St. Benedict had steadily supplanted the Celtic custom everywhere. It had reached Wessex even in St. Aldhelm's days, and Dunstan's reforms had made it the universal monastic Rule throughout England. Monastic missions now became exceptional, and the monks of Wessex henceforth stayed at home. The Rule made each monastery a self-sufficient unit, in which each monk must wholly sink his own identity. He submitted himself to the Rule and to his abbot, vowing poverty, chastity and obedience, and remaining in the monastery of his profession until superior orders or death released him. Pastoral work among the laity was now left to the parish priests under their archdeacons and bishops, who were later to share it with the Mendicant Friars. The monks henceforth turned inwards on themselves, devoting their lives to the divine services in the monastery church, the management of their buildings and estates, and the labours, both manual and scholarly, imposed upon them by the Rule. Formal charity absorbed a small part of their income, but they did not undertake general poor relief. They kept no schools for the laity, though they educated their own novices and sometimes trained the sons of wealthy neighbours. The monastery had become an end in itself, its members withdrawn from the world and unconcerned with it, in their search for perfection in communion with God.

Yet they continued profoundly to influence life in the West, as throughout the Christian world. Withdrawal was an ideal realizable only in part: the world was with them even inside the monastery walls. Monasteries and nunneries multiplied as wealthy benefactors, zealous to promote the Christian way of life, endowed new houses. New orders, Cluniac, Cistercian, Carthusian, Gilbertine, Augustinian and others, each a characteristic variation on the original Benedictine theme, came in turn and flourished. The Benedictine nunneries of Shaftesbury, Wilton and Romsey, the Augustinian canonesses of Lacock, and many other nunneries too, shared in this expansion, bringing their special contribution in the minor arts of copying and needlework, for which some of them made England famous. In the seven western shires there were nearly a hundred houses, great and small. In Gloucestershire they were so numerous that some have thought this the explanation of the old proverb, "As sure as God's in Gloucestershire." Others consider it a reference to the phial of the Holy Blood which Henry III's brother brought from Germany to enrich his Cistercian foundation at Hailes.

Nobles vied with kings in heaping wealth upon the monasteries which they took under their patronage, watching with pride the growth and rebuilding, in ever more lavish styles, of the great churches where their ancestors lay buried and where they, too, in turn, would be laid. In the later Middle Ages they endowed the monasteries with rich manors to maintain chantry-priests to say perpetual masses for their souls, in the exquisite little chantry chapels which now began to embellish the chancels and transepts of the great churches. Where in all England, save at Westminster, can we see a cluster of chantry chapels to match the splendid and delicate beauty of those which adorn Tewkesbury's chancel, like a blaze of glorious jewels in a queen's diadem? In this mausoleum of the nobility of medieval England, a veritable Westminster of the West in the profusion of its famous dead, the names of the barons who lie there in their tombs are a roll-call of English chivalry—Robert fitz Hamo, the Norman founder of the abbey, four successive generations of the Clare earls of Gloucester, five generations of Despensers after them, the Beauchamps, Beauforts, Courtenays and many another, and finally Edward, Prince of Wales, butchered in the battle just beyond the abbey, and his slayer and cousin, George, Duke of Clarence, himself executed for treason a few years later.

As heavily endowed perpetual corporations, the monasteries had to learn estate management. The Rule had prescribed daily manual labour for all monks, thus upholding the dignity of work in days when snobbery and pride were all too prone to think it fit only for serfs. But now it was much relaxed in practice. Nevertheless, shrewd abbots applied their minds to financing and managing estates, and to technical farming problems, and in the twelfth and thirteenth centuries, the monks taught England, both by practical example and by theoretical treatises, how to drain the marshes, control the floods, increase the yield and quality of corn, and so organize estates as to produce a surplus of food for markets in the rising towns. Pioneers in cattle-breeding and especially in sheep-rearing, monasteries like Winchester, Cirencester, Winchcomb, Gloucester and Tewkesbury had thousands of sheep on the short, sweet grass of the Cotswolds, the Mendips, and Salisbury Plain. Their wool was the finest in Europe, and wealthy merchants from Italy and Flanders competed keenly to buy it for the looms of Florence, Milan or Ghent.

In architecture, they shared the lead with the great secular cathedrals, using their revenues to engage famous professional architects to design their buildings, and scores of skilled craftsmen and unskilled labourers to erect them. Gloucester, Tewkesbury, Malmesbury, Romsey, Christchurch and Winchester show us still the new Norman style introduced by Norman abbots, massive, secure, orderly and self-confident, even if its majesty is earthbound and rude. The choir of Winchester, the ruins of Tintern and Glastonbury, exemplify the purest of all medieval styles, the Early English, delicate and graceful, relying on line and proportion to represent perfectly in stone the devotion, self-surrender and aspiration so proper to a monastery. Before 1340 the monks of Gloucester saw the marvellous Perpendicular style created for their south transept and their choir. The most English of all medieval styles, it spread from Gloucester everywhere in the fifteenth century, capturing the fashion with its confident vertical lines, its noble transoms, its superb blaze of vast windows, and its miraculous fan-vaulting, another Gloucester invention, like intricate lace-work frozen into stone.

Learning, however, had passed to the rising universities after 1200. Although Glastonbury, Winchester and other houses still had great libraries and frequently added to them, the western monks did not even continue the great tradition of chronicle-writing established centuries earlier, at Winchester, when at King Alfred's orders the Anglo-Saxon Chronicle was begun. The oldest and greatest vernacular Chronicle in Europe, it perished when the Norman Conquest degraded English into a peasant patois, nor did any great Latin chronicle arise in the West to replace it, though at Glastonbury William of Malmesbury laboured, not without success, to emulate, in his great history of the Norman kings, the qualities of method, style and outlook of his great model, Bede.

But Glastonbury now acquired a different fame, far transcending any with which sober history, tied to facts, could ever crown her: she became the centre of the noblest of all myths, the legend of Arthur and the quest of the Holy Grail. When Geoffrey of Monmouth popularized his Norman-Christian version of these ancient Celtic legends, so that within a few years the courtly and the educated worlds were bemused with the romance of Arthur and his knights, where else should Arthur's unknown grave be found—when, whether for political or for financial reasons, found it had to be— than at Glastonbury, oldest of all the monasteries of England, with its ancient glory of pious legend woven into its unbroken history stretching back into the twilit days when Arthur and his knights had fought against the pagan foes of God and Britain? Despite pedantic sceptics who demanded facts and derided fakes, the legend took root and flourished, and within a few generations the whole story, with Joseph of Arimathea, the Holy Grail, the famous thorn and all the rest of it, was so firmly rooted in Glastonbury tradition that not even the Reformation could tear it out.

So the monks played their part in society. Their abbots rode often to Parliament at Westminster, or sat as judges in local courts. In wartime, they sent the King the feudal service due from their lands. As local landowners, they encountered their neighbours and tenants, high and low, in daily business. And through the centuries they daily discharged their most sacred duty, the *Opus Dei*, the rhythm of divine services in the Church. The Psalmist had said, "Seven times a day do I praise thee for thy righteous judgments, and at midnight will I rise to give thee thanks." St. Benedict had therefore decreed the canonical hours of Matins, Lauds, Prime, Tierce, Sext, None, Evensong and Compline, to fill the day with praise. To this duty all else was incidental and subordinate: for this ritual their churches were designed: to heighten its solemnity they were made splendid with all that the Rule would allow and piety bestow. To the last, the *Opus Dei* remained the true purpose of monastic life.

I will not dwell upon their failings, for I seek only to describe their work. In time, the bright flame of their early fervour paled and died. They no longer laboured in the fields, they dressed and fed well, evading the strictness of the Rule by pitiful subterfuges. Some houses virtually became comfortable residential clubs for elderly, selfish bachelors, monks in name but not in spirit, living on the accumulated endowments of past ages. Their administration and finance became feeble and chaotic, their numbers dwindled and discipline decayed. When the Dissolution came, it was time that they should go; they had outlived their noble heritage.

Yet not even the most Protestant or the most rationalist of us can read unmoved the story of the trial and execution of Richard Whiting, the last of the long line of Abbots of Glastonbury. We in our own days have seen too many of these tragic clashes between the almighty secular State claiming absolute obedience in the name of the people, and the inflexible prelate standing for his own conception of the law of God and the right of his Church, not to understand clearly and poignantly the implications of this unequal duel. Doubtless the old man had concealed the sacred treasures of his house from the King's avid inquisitors: doubtless he had hoped that the good old days would come back again, and he may well have schemed to use money, gold and jewels to speed that return by conspiracy and rebellion if need be. But most certainly he was brought to trial on trumped-up charges by men who had determined the verdict and the sentence before ever they had framed the indictment, and who twisted his words and actions, and played upon popular envy and resentment to weave a cloak of legality, hiding the nakedness of their intent. So, on a November day in 1539, the abbot, as steadfast in spirit as he was infirm in body, was dragged through the streets of his town to the top of its stark Tor, baited all the way with a rain of questions urging him to implicate his "accomplices", and when these failed to wring any admission from him, he was at last hanged with all the hideous ceremony of a brutal and cruel age.

The needless violence, greed, prejudice and slander of the royal agents who executed the task cast a halo of martyrdom over the end of the monks, obscuring the fact that the death sentences, shocking as they were, were most exceptional. The vast majority of monks and nuns returned to secular life with adequate pensions or with church livings in appropriate cases. Over this episode controversy has long raged, alike among scholars and propagandists on either side: we will remember, not the pitiful end, but the glorious beginning and the mighty labours of the monks of the West.

VI

The Making of the Landscape

by

W. G. HOSKINS

IF one stands on some commanding hill almost anywhere in Devon, away from the moors, one looks out
over an immense landscape quite unlike that of the
Midlands—a landscape of thousands of coloured fields
and woods—most of the fields very small, irregular in
shape, shut in by massive hedge-banks which are often
faced with great blocks of native stone; and on top of
these hedge-banks tall trees—sycamore, oak, ash and
elm—grow freely.

Between these high, mounded hedges runs a network
of lanes, linking together by slender threads the lonely
farms scattered about the flanks or shoulders of the
hills, or half-buried among the trees at the bottom of
some little combe. Here and there, in a more favoured
and sheltered spot, a hamlet of three or four farmsteads
with its cottages clusters round a grey church tower:
but there is rarely a village to be seen even in the widest

view. It is a landscape of hamlets and isolated farms, not of large, compact villages like the Midlands.

This fundamental difference between the Midland landscape and that of South-Western England shows up very strikingly in aerial photographs, from which the historian can learn a great deal—particularly the pre-historian looking at aerial photographs of the moorlands or the downlands—but this is a separate subject altogether. I am concerned this evening with the landscape that was created by the Anglo-Saxon and medieval farmers, the landscape we see to-day.

In the Midlands, too, the fields are generally much larger—and they are much more regular in shape—straight hedges with right-angled corners, all very tidy—and dull. There are none of those great hedge-banks crowned by large timber: only thin hedges of quickset growing straight out of the ground. And there are few lanes in the Midland landscape—nothing that a Devonshire man would call a lane, anyway—only straight, open by-roads with wide grass verges, open to every wind that blows.

For the most part, the Midland landscape is the result of an orderly and deliberate planning, nearly all done between one hundred and fifty and two hundred years ago—the work of the commissioners and surveyors who carried out the enclosure of hundreds of English parishes under a set procedure.

Maps were carefully prepared, new roads planned on them, new hedge-lines sketched in, obliterating the older pattern that had been there since Saxon and medieval times. It was all done on paper first, and done very efficiently and quickly. But it is an artificial and comparatively modern landscape, and that is what is wrong with it, what makes it so unsatisfying, so unappealing to anybody born in the far west, beyond the Somerset plain.

For this is where the true, ancient landscape of South-Western England begins—where the neck of the peninsula is narrowest, where the ramparts of Blackdown and Quantock rise up ahead of us, and every detail of the scene begins to change. The speech of the people changes, the size of the fields and their shape, the kind of hedges, the lanes. Villages disappear. Isolated farmsteads take their place—often with massive walls of grey stone, coloured by lichens, like rustic fortresses built round a courtyard with all the windows facing inwards on to the yard. These isolated, lonely farmsteads are ancient—older than the Norman Conquest many of them, their names written in Domesday Book. Few of the others are less than seven hundred years old. Four out of every five farms in this part of England were here before the Black Death came to put a stop to the great colonizing movement of the western wastelands. It is an old, unplanned landscape—unplanned in every way. It has grown like this over several centuries; it is not the creation of a few men working on paper with preconceived ideas.

It began to take shape dimly in the seventh and

eighth centuries, and the pattern was practically completed by the middle of the fourteenth. Only a little tidying-up remained to be done in later generations on the higher ground.

And in the main it is the creation of countless thousands of anonymous peasant farmers and small squires. It is they who had drawn the map of South-Western England before 1350. They had filled in nearly all the names on the map by then; and they had drawn in, one by one, slowly and laboriously, all the fields, the lanes, the farmsteads, the little parks and the manor-houses, the bridges and the small grey churches of rubble masonry out of the local quarry.

This, indeed, is the secret history of the West, as secret as its little hidden combes and streams themselves. We have to find our clues to the silent process of colonization where we can—in the private muniments of those old families who have lived in the same place since the twelfth century, some of whom still remain, and in monastic records of the same period. Then there is the Ordnance map, one of the richest documents we have for our early history; and the landscape itself, which can be made to yield many clues as to what happened in the dark centuries before and after the Norman Conquest.

The Anglo-Saxons began the conquest and settlement of Devon in the year 658. By the end of the seventh century they had probably occupied all the country east of the Exe; and within the next century

or so they occupied the rest of the county as far as the
Tamar. How much Celtic settlement they found is still
a matter of dispute. The evidence of the place-names
of Devon, which are overwhelmingly Anglo-Saxon in
derivation, and less than one per cent pre-English, sug-
gests that the old English invaders found themselves in
an almost completely virgin landscape of moor and
heath, forest and marsh.

And so the enormous task of clearing these great
tracts of countryside—mostly forested with oak and
ash; or true moorland like Dartmoor, Exmoor and
Bodmin Moor; or heath country like the Blackdowns—
so this great task began. Yard by yard, acre by acre,
field by field, that immense, well-cultivated landscape
we see from our Devonian heights has been painfully
cleared—cleared of millions of tons of surface stone, of
hundreds of thousands of great trees, of mountains of
brushwood and undergrowth. No wonder it took seven
hundred years or so to accomplish.

The colonization of the South-West went on slowly
between the seventh century and the eleventh. By 1066
there were, in Devon alone, some twelve hundred settlements in existence—a handful of towns, a large number
of villages, and a much greater number of hamlets and
solitary farmsteads. There was a very even spread over
almost the entire country, on good and bad soils alike;
though Devon in general was much more thinly peopled
than Somerset to the east—and as one went west into
Cornwall the settlements and population grew even

sparser. Even so, isolated farmsteads were to be found in the eleventh century up to eleven or twelve hundred feet on the eastern side of Dartmoor, and up to nine hundred feet on the wetter, more exposed western slopes. We haven't gone any higher than this to-day, except in very few places.

But the process of clearing and bringing the virgin land into use was still far from completed. It is probable that from a third to a half of Devon was still uncultivated land, even outside Dartmoor, and in Cornwall there was even more waste. Thousands of farms on the map to-day were still not known in 1086.

The work went on after the Conquest with gathering impetus, possibly after a long pause until the great revolution in the countryside—for such it was—was safely over. New farms and hamlets came into being in the twelfth century; smoke rose from new clearings in the dwindling woods, and the swallows found their way to barns hitherto unknown; and the older settlements slowly extended their own boundaries, pushing back the encircling forest and the heath and moor, and draining the marshes.

There is good evidence of this steady expansion in the twelfth century in the hundreds of little churches that were first built in these years—especially between about 1150 and 1220. Most of the country churches of Devon and Cornwall are plain little fifteenth-century buildings in their outward appearance—but if one pushes open the door and steps inside, the Norman font is there as the silent witness to a far older building on the site. There are well over a hundred of these Norman fonts still left in Devon—many more must have been replaced—and over eighty left in Cornwall. Most of them can be dated late in the twelfth century, and we can well imagine from their style that they were made in the time of the learned Bartholomew of Exeter, who reigned over the diocese of Exeter—which then extended from the borders of Somerset down to Land's End—from 1161 to 1184. He was one of Exeter's greatest bishops, and not the least of his contributions to the life of the West was the vigorous creation of hundreds of new parishes, with their homely little churches built by local men with local stone, stone from their own fields.

After the disafforestation of Devon in 1204—for which the men of Devon paid King John five thousand marks—the pace of new settlement increased rapidly.

Thousands of new farms came into being in the five generations between 1204 and 1348, when the Black Death stopped it all. The great majority of Devon and Cornish farms first appear in the records in these years. Only a few date from later centuries, and those chiefly in the upland country where much waste land survived until the seventeenth and eighteenth centuries.

Many of these farmsteads were so isolated from the parish church in the Middle Ages that they received licences from the bishop to celebrate divine service in their own chapels. The great parish of Hartland had more than a dozen of these chapels scattered over its length and breadth; many parishes had three or four. One frequently comes across these chapels to this day—generally in a separate building in the farmyard, now used as a barn or a stable, but still clearly recognizable. I was in one only the other day on a farm in Colebrooke parish, where up in the hay-loft the fourteenth-century roof of the chapel of Blessed Mary was still intact.

The fields of the South-West are small—many of them only an acre or two—because they were taken in from the moor and the forest by the medieval peasant or his Anglo-Saxon forebears with primitive plough, or even more painfully dug with a spade alone. The hedge-banks are high and massive because they had to keep wild animals away from the stock, or give shelter to stock and crops—especially in Cornwall and west Devon where the salt Atlantic winds stunt even the trees. And the lanes between the high banks, twisting up the hillsides from one peasant farm to the next, because they, too, were hacked out yard by yard and grew planlessly and painfully, going round large trees or massive boulders, taking any course that would save a day's labour, and yet arriving at their destination in the end.

There is, of course, a great deal more one could say about all this: I have left many questions unanswered. But it is time to say a little about the men who created this landscape.

Most of the isolated farms and hamlets were settled

from the beginning by peasant landowners who were granted their lands on nominal terms by their overlords in order to encourage the clearing and reclamation of the waste. All over Devon, for example, we find hundreds of farm-names which compound old English personal names with *hayes,* or *hayne,* or *worthy*—clearly small, enclosed farms held in severalty from the beginning.

These first settlers, clearing their land of stones and timber acre by acre, gradually created farms of thirty to fifty acres or so in the space of perhaps two or three generations; and there they stayed for centuries, either giving their names to their farms or taking their names from them—like Docton of Docton, Fursdon of Fursdon, thousands of them altogether—probably a few in every parish in Devon and Cornwall. From these ancient freeholders of the twelfth and thirteenth centuries—some of them may indeed have come right through the Norman Conquest from some Old English thane—sprang in later generations many a great family in Church and State. These ancient farmsteads became the nursery and seed-plot of great men, of whom Devon and Cornwall were to produce so many, men who were able to devote their lives and their talents to the State because they enjoyed the quiet possession of well-cultivated estates which had been hacked so slowly out of the primeval wilderness by their forefathers in bygone centuries.

E

VII

Tudor Cornwall
by
A. L. ROWSE

Cornwall in the Middle Ages was a little land very
much on its own, living its own inner life wrapt up in
its own Celtic tongue, in its dream of the Celtic past,
rather a backwater, a dead-end. As the great Bishop
Grandison wrote to his friends, the Pope and cardinals
at their gay, sunny court by the Rhone at Avignon—
"And beyond is nothing but the great sundering flood."
We are apt to forget that in the Middle Ages this was
not only the land's end but the end of the world.

The Tudor period—roughly the sixteenth century—
changed all that. It was then that the New World
beyond the Atlantic was discovered and the voyages
set in being to open it up and plant colonies there.
This was the making of England's fortune: that is why
that time has such an extreme importance in our history: it started the process of making the island into a
world power.

67

The effect of this on Cornwall was decisive: from being a remote little backwater the extreme West—Cornwall and Devon—found themselves flung into the front line of all the Atlantic developments—fisheries, trade, ocean voyages, war: they were in the country's front line in the long struggle with Spain, the Armada and all the rest of it. Cornwall was, in a way, transformed by it. That transformation is my theme.

Naturally the little backward society reacted against these new pulls and forces, as such societies usually do. Not that it does them any good. The reaction took the form of a couple of rebellions: two in the year 1497, which may count as two waves of the same movement, and half a century later the Prayer Book Rebellion of 1549—of which we celebrate the quater-centenary this year. These two rebellions have the same significance in West Country history as the Jacobite Rebellions of 1715 and 1745 for Scotland: the last kicks of an out-of-date mode of life and society against the inevitable. We should know as much about the '97 and the '49, and remember them better, if they were not so long ago: they made a great stir in the land in their own day and a great upheaval here in the West.

The first rising, by the way, was against taxation—I don't know if there is not something congenial in that idea—the Cornish objected to being taxed to pay for the defence of the frontier against the Scots. They rose in their thousands under the leadership of a powerful blacksmith from the Lizard area, Michael Joseph, and a plausible lawyer from Bodmin, Thomas Flamank. Gathering supporters as they marched up through Devon and Somerset, the rebels arrived in view of London, unchecked, and camped on Blackheath. There was consternation in the city; the Queen and the Archbishop of Canterbury took refuge in the Tower.

The King marched out and defeated them; though it is nice to think that the Cornish bowmen gave a good account of themselves with their long bows, and their leader, Michael Joseph, went to his death at Tyburn in high spirit and unabashed. He boasted that he should "have a name perpetual, and a fame permanent and immortal"—as in a way he has. The Cornish were undaunted by their defeat, and rose again in the autumn under the lead of Perkin Warbeck. They got as far as Wells before they were dispersed. This time the King made them pay heavily for their jollifications: they did not do it again for half a century.

But in 1549 the West rose against the imposition of the English Prayer Book: the rising began in Devon and was joined by the Cornish. It was probably concerted, as it was led, by the priests. It was the last kick of the medieval Catholic order in the West against the new religious order—the other wing in the progressive forward march of the sixteenth century. The rising was a serious affair: it kept the government paralysed during that summer; Exeter was besieged and held out for a whole month within its walls—that rich commercial and religious capital would have made excellent plunder for hungry rebels; but Lord Russell came to the rescue with German mercenaries, and the rising was suppressed with a good deal of bloodshed. Cornwall suffered severely; but that was the end: she gave no more trouble.

Henceforward Cornwall and Devon played their part in the new movements of the age, on land and sea, with spirit and ardour—and to their profit. It is fascinating to watch the process in detail—as I have tried to do in my book *Tudor Cornwall*. There is first the change-over in religion, from a Catholic basis, static, timeless, universal, to a Protestant basis, progressive, energetic, nationalist. You see, it is a part of the change involving the whole society. The monasteries, which had out-lived their usefulness and become old, inefficient abuses, were dissolved. In place of the squabbling and indolent canons of Launceston, Bodmin, St. Germans, Tywar-dreath, you get the active and pushing new gentry exploiting the land to full capacity, investing their capital and making better use of it: John Eliot makes Port Eliot out of St. Germans, the Carews cultivate Launceston priory lands, John Rashleigh of Fowey, to the fore in commerce. His son sails his ship, the *Frances* of Fowey, under Drake against the Armada; he takes the place of bibulous old Prior Collins of Tywardreath, slowly soaking in his study in the priory there in that sunny valley looking out to sea. A new age has dawned: the leadership has passed to newer, more active, forward spirits!

70

They see that our future is on the sea, and here the great development in the farthest West takes place. This is the age of the fame and ascendancy of Plymouth, whence so many of the voyages, not only the most famous of Hawkins and Drake, set out. In the course of the long war with Spain, Plymouth became our front-line fortress. It was now, too, that Falmouth took its first rise : we find some celebrated ships coming in and out of harbour there, and some celebrated persons too—like Sir Walter Raleigh and the dashing, tragic Earl of Essex.

Naturally these new developments brought up with them the new Protestant seafaring families that were sympathetic to them.

The old Catholic families went down : the Arundells of Lanherne, for example—you can still see their beautiful Tudor house, now a convent, at St. Mawgan; the senior line of the Courtenays, Earls of Devon, came to an end. But at Plymouth the new families of Hawkins and Drake came up; and Drake settled himself at Buckland Abbey which he bought from Sir Richard Grenville with some of the proceeds of his raid on the Spanish treasure-route off the coast of Peru. You can still see that house, made by the Grenvilles out of the original abbey church : in its way a precise and visual epitome of the transformation of the age. Other West Country families that took to the sea and Protestantism did well out of it : Raleighs, Grenvilles, Killigrews, Carews, Tremaynes. We notice them very much to

the fore in public affairs and at Court. The brilliant
court of Queen Elizabeth had a strong West Country
contingent very much entrenched there: Sir Walter
Raleigh, one of her handsomest and closest favourites,
who "spake broad Devonshire to his dying day";
William Killigrew, one of her intimate servants as
groom of the Privy Chamber; his brother, Sir Henry
Killigrew, a leading diplomat; Edmund Tremayne, for
long Clerk of the Privy Council, a very eminent civil
servant.

The fact is that Devon and Cornwall became much
more important than they had been before—particularly Cornwall—as the result of the West coming into
the forefront of national affairs. And this gives us the
clue to what people have very much wondered about—
why it was that Cornwall got such an enormous number
of Members of Parliament, forty-four altogether. Most
of these seats were created during the Tudor period:
some of them perhaps because they were convenient for
the return of official members, others because the leading gentry wanted to sit in Parliament, whereas previously people wished to avoid that unpleasant and
expensive duty.

It was convenient for Sir Francis Drake, for example,
to be returned for Boscastle—which I do not suppose
he ever saw—and a very good House of Commons man
he made, sitting on many committees: he evidently
had the confidence of the House as a man of affairs. In
fact the Cornish members were as independent as any

others—some of them more so; and in the next generation Cornwall contributed, in Sir John Eliot, the leader
in Parliament's opposition to the Crown. Here we are
on the threshold of the Civil War.

Perhaps I may put in proper perspective another
historical misconception while I am about it. Many
people have the idea that after the Reformation the
Church neglected Cornwall and failed to make any impression until Wesley came along. That is entirely
wrong—in fact nonsense. The Church was as active
in Cornwall, as essential a part of society, as anywhere
else: its work went on in the parishes through the centuries. A fair number of Cornish families held out
against the new order as Catholic Recusants, sending
their children abroad to be educated, some of them
returning to become martyrs for the old Faith. But
they were a small minority: the great bulk of people
went along with the new deal in Church and State.

This undoubtedly brought with it a great increase of
wealth for the country and better conditions for the
people. Better houses, better food, increased production from the soil, more chances in the world: this was
generally true all over England. Life in the Middle
Ages was very bare and hard, poverty-stricken and serf-
like for most people; the Elizabethan Age was one of
increasing wealth and comfort. Cornwall was no
exception: Carew notices that Cornish agriculture saw
a great improvement; houses began to have ceilings and
windows of glass, people to have somewhat better fare:

73

previously they had lived on "Whitsul"—milk and cheese, fish and barley or rye-bread, very little meat. Fishing played a much more important part in those days, and it was at this time that the new development of seine-fishing came in. Tin was the one industry of Cornwall that distinguished it among counties, and the Tudor period saw two marked developments: the eastward shift of the industry from Devon to Cornwall, and from east Cornwall to west, which now took the leading place. Here the Godolphins were pioneers, brought in German mining experts to advise, employed some hundreds of men. It was Sir Francis Godolphin who gave Carew the remarkable account of the industry that he put into his *Survey of Cornwall*, that most delightful of all Elizabethan county surveys. Secondly, there was the shift over from tin-streaming to tin-mining, with the exhaustion of alluvial deposits and the following up of the lodes into the hillsides and cliffs. Little did those Tudor miners, whose workings we may still come upon in waste places, know the great extension to come of their industry in the nineteenth century and the use of the inherited skill of their descendants, the Cornish miners, all over the world.

VIII

The Western Sea
by
JAMES A. WILLIAMSON

MIDDLE-WEST Americans and prairie Canadians may live unconscious of the sea. But to Englishmen, even of the Midlands, the sea is ever present, not far over the sky-line, two or three hours on modern wheels, a couple of days' riding in the slow times of old. It is in our business calculations, our public policies and our adventurous thoughts; and it has been for centuries.

Much more so has it been to West Countrymen. They are between the two coasts of the English Channel and the Bristol Channel. Their country is a triangle with two long sea sides and a short land base, only sixty miles from Bristol to Southampton Water. And as the triangle narrows westward the two seas draw nearer to all.

The sea brought the population to the West Country. The Iberian stock, some of the Celts, and the West Saxons landed directly on the western coasts. It brought their enemies, also, the Viking Danes and raiders from France and Spain. It brought their earliest economic visitors, the Phoenicians, who came for western tin, and the Armorican Gauls whose stout ships moved Caesar to admiration.

As the West Country consolidated, its people began to trade back. Geography gave them almost a monopoly of trade with Ireland, and early Bristol rose to prominence mainly on the strength of it. There were trades with western France, Spain and Portugal. All these trades are older than history, and no one knows when they began. The western fishermen went to the Irish coast and the cod fishery of Iceland, where Bristol men were at work in the fifteenth century.

The southern coast is one of natural harbours, safe and well distributed. Southampton was only twelve miles from the Saxon capital of Winchester. It was a naval port for the Plantagenet kings. Henry V built ships in Southampton Water, and thence he sailed to Agincourt. A century later Henry Huttoft, the Southampton merchant, built the *Great Harry* for the Tudor king. Southampton's trade expanded in the Middle Ages until the port was the greatest in England, after London. It monopolized the spice trade with the Italian city-states, and its landlocked waters harboured Venetian galleasses and Genoese carracks, discharging the richest wares in the world. Then came decline. The Mediterranean trade died out when the Cape route to India was found, and Southampton fell into decay.

The King's service also deserted it, and Henry VII made Portsmouth his naval base and built there the first dry dock in England, while Henry VIII fortified Portsmouth and watched his navy fight the French at Spithead in 1545.

Farther west, Poole achieved a different fame. It was the home port of Harry Pay, the master pirate of the fifteenth century, whose fleets ranged the Channel to the cost of France and Spain. Down Channel lay Exeter, the capital of the West. It was miles up a narrow waterway, but had a large foreign trade and a Company of Merchant Adventurers giving an outlet to the West Country cloth industry. Dartmouth was more accessible, its entrance guarded by twin castles, its deep waters within allowing ships to ride close to the streets. Dartmouth was for Chaucer the typical western port, the home of his sea captain with the tempest-shaken beard.

Plymouth was at first a fishing village on the shore of Sutton Pool, growing slowly into a town of foreign trade. We hear little of the usual company regulation of Plymouth's merchants, for the Plymouth men were individualists, and individual enterprise by the Hawkinses and Drake put Plymouth in the first rank in Tudor times. Then, also, the Navy came westwards and made Plymouth its base for fighting Spain, to the detriment of Portsmouth, which was deserted by the Navy in Elizabeth's reign.

Fowey was another deep-water estuary, a smaller

version of Dartmouth, its entrance only a bowshot over between the forts. It, too, had its great days when the "gallants of Fowey" lorded it over all the Channel, and traded, fought, and plundered as they pleased. Like all such lords of violence, they overdid it, and at length Edward IV took them in hand. His hand was heavy, and he left them wiser men.

Round the Land's End the northern shore was different from the southern. All the way up to Bristol there were no safe and easy harbours, but shoal and difficult inlets, poor refuges from a gale-swept sea. Their people, however, braved all, with their fishing and coasting trade, but none of the ports grew to the first magnitude. Tennyson speaks of the *Revenge* as manned from "Bideford in Devon", but Bideford was a small place to find the two or three hundred men required. The Bristol Channel, in fact, was primarily the sea that led to Bristol, which had all the natural gifts for greatness.

This port of Bristol, landlocked, safe, and defensible, had open water to the ocean and little more than a hundred miles to go by land to London. In the Middle Ages, when the ocean was yet mysterious, the Bristol men had a network of trade with Ireland, western France, and Portugal and Spain. But the ocean called them. They went out west of Ireland, looking for new lands: the Island of Brasil, the Island of the Seven Cities, the Fortunate Islands of St. Brandan. Then, as the Tudor period opened, a stranger came to

Bristol with a plan that fired their hearts. He was John Cabot from Venice, and in effect he said: Let us leave casting to and fro for islands which we always miss, and press on due west until we hit something. That something will be Cathay, where the spices grow. They will make you as rich as Venice and richer than Southampton. Give me a ship, and I will show you.

They gave him a ship, the *Matthew* of Bristol. He sailed in April 1497, and was back in August, having discovered, as he said, Cathay. It was really North America, but none guessed that such a continent existed. They all thought it must be the coast of Asia.

And so disappointment followed, for North America was a savage land with no spices. But Bristol persevered, and in a few years had a company at work, the first corporation in English history for trans-oceanic trade, called the Company Adventurers to the New Found Land. What those adventurers did and where they went is all a mystery. In after years it was a Bristol claim that Robert Thorne and Hugh Elyot were "the discoverers of the New Found Land".

The Company declined and died, but something permanent remained—the Newfoundland fishery. The Bristol men, and all the West Country seamen, worked it for centuries, almost to our own time. In the spring the little ships sailed from the western ports, fished and salted or dried their catch, and came home at the end of summer. It was called "a gainful trade", for it brought in more wealth than it took out. The great fishery had also a high place in the national defence, since it trained seamen for the Navy. In Stuart times ten thousand men went yearly to Newfoundland; and these men were all at home in the winter, available for the Navy if the King's enemies threatened trouble. Truly a gainful trade!

Bristol made other links with the West. She took part in planting the infant American colonies, and a greater part in trading with them when they grew up. Colonial tobacco and sugar and rum caused her to build refineries and factories; and so grew the modern Bristol of industry and trade combined.

It was in the Tudor period that Plymouth became an oceanic port. William Hawkins sailed his Plymouth ships to South America in the reign of Henry VIII. He opened the Brazil trade, whose chief product in those days was not nuts but dyestuffs for the use of England's cloth industry.

The Hawkinses were prominent for a century, three generations of them, of whom the greatest was Sir John Hawkins, the merchant-diplomatist, the sea-father of Drake, and the administrator who made the Navy fit to beat the Armada. Plymouth worships Drake, the genius of his age, but she ought not to forget John Hawkins, one of those men who do great work and say little about it.

And Plymouth, like Bristol, maintained her touch with colonization and discovery. On her waterside are two memorial stones, one commemorating the departure of the Pilgrim Fathers in the *Mayflower* in 1620, the other the sailing of the good ship *Tory* in 1839 with the pioneer settlers of New Zealand. It was not the first connection with New Zealand, for Captain Cook had sailed from Plymouth on all the three great voyages which opened the Pacific to the modern world.

The warlike eighteenth century developed both Plymouth and Portsmouth. The Navy, a visitor to Plymouth in Tudor and Stuart times, became a resident in the great French wars, when the dockyard took shape on the lowest reach of the Tamar and was later christened Devonport. And just as Drake stands for Plymouth in the roll of the Admirals, so Nelson is linked with Portsmouth, which bade him farewell as he sailed for Trafalgar.

Amid the great ports the minor ones should not be forgotten. Blake won fame by his defence of Lyme Regis, Wolfe embarked at Lymington for his conquest of Quebec, while even little Beaulieu River on the edge of the New Forest built ships like the famous *Agamemnon* for Nelson's fleet.

As for Falmouth, its wonderful natural harbour was little used in earlier times. But with the growth of ocean trade it found its function, first as a terminus for swift-sailing mail-packets to America, and second as a port of call for homeward-bound merchantmen in the nineteenth century.

Such vessels, from the East Indies or Australia, had been months at sea out of touch with their owners. As they drew near the Channel their captains could not know at which port in England or the Continent their goods would be required, and so they put into Falmouth for telegraphic news. "Falmouth for orders" became the destination of many a great sailing-ship until the sailing-ships died out, and steamers and radio changed the conditions of ocean trade.

Up Channel, Southampton waited long for revival to the status of a first-class port. In the nineteenth century revival came, when the passenger steamers and the railway link with London placed Southampton Water on the changing map of the trade-routes. The new importance of Southampton began with the P. and O. liners in the early Victorian time. The London and South Western Railway afterwards enlarged the docks, and Southampton in our day takes its place as the terminal port for the greatest vessels of modern times, the liners whose names are household words to all.

Large and small, the ports have all played their part in West-Country life, in fishing and trade alike. Fowey earns dollars by shipping china clay, and Brixham, the pioneer of modern trawling, has but changed in recent memory from brown sails to diesel engines. Methods alter, but character persists; and to seek new enterprise was always in the character of the western seamen.

IX

The Civil War in the West

by

PROFESSOR J. SIMMONS

THERE are several different ways of looking at the
history of the English Civil War. The national historian, who is considering the war as a whole, concerns
himself chiefly with the great issues it was fought over,
with the authority of King and Parliament: he sees it
as the climax of a long struggle for political power. The
local historian, on the other hand, looks at it another
way. Of course he has always got these great issues in
his mind, but to him it is first of all a local story. He
is concerned not with the debates at Westminster and
Oxford, not with the great armies and their commanders, except when for a brief moment they may
irrupt into the country he is writing about. No: his
business is with smaller things, with personal jealousies
and rivalries, with country-house warfare, with the raising and maintenance of small forces, which act loosely
together and often fall apart at critical moments of

victory or defeat. But it is this microscopic examination, I think, that keeps us closest to the minds of the people who fought in the war themselves. Some of them, the most resolute and clear-sighted, took up arms for principles they firmly held: far more, the great majority, fought out of personal attachment to a landlord, or a general loyalty to the King; or they fought from fear of Popery, or dislike of a neighbour, or—passive and against their will—because they were pressed into service.

In the West Country the Civil War has an interest all its own. For one thing, it has been described by contemporaries more fully and intimately than the war in any other part of England. Clarendon was himself in the West for the last two years, and in the ninth book of his great *History of the Rebellion* he gives an unforgettable account of the whole business as he watched it in 1645 and 1646. The best of the Royalist commanders, Hopton, has left us his own story of the campaign he waged; and from the other side there is a day-to-day account of Fairfax's operations, which brought the war in the West to an end, written by one of the chaplains in his army. And then on top of this a vast mass, a mountain, of letters and pamphlets survives. As you work through it you come to feel you know the men who were engaged in the war, what they fought for, why they lost or won.

In the West, as elsewhere, it is broadly true to say that the peers and the greater gentry stood on the

King's side, the lesser gentry and the townsmen for
Parliament. Yet there were great exceptions. At Bristol
and Exeter the townsmen were deeply divided: the
Royalists there represented a very large minority. The
gentry of East Somerset were on the whole Parliamentarian—Horners and Pophams and so on. And the
steady Royalism of Cornwall was tempered by the grim,
unyielding Puritanism of the Lord Robartes, with his
great power in the centre of the county.

The war began in 1642. At the end of July the Mar-
quess of Hertford arrived in Somerset, with the King's
commission as Lieutenant-General to levy forces for his
defence. He took up his quarters at Wells, but he soon
found that countryside hostile and thought it prudent
to withdraw, after managing to raise no more than five
hundred troops. He went first to Sherborne and then,
as his position became more and more difficult, he determined to cross over into South Wales to join up with
the King in the West Midlands. He left behind him
as his deputy Sir Ralph Hopton, Member of Parliament for Wells. Hopton's position was extremely difficult. The general feeling of Somerset and Devon was
so far strongly in favour of Parliament. It was plain he
could attempt nothing useful there for the present, and
he accordingly retired into Cornwall. There in a few
weeks, with the aid of Sir Bevil Grenville and a few
other determined supporters of the King, he succeeded
in raising a respectable force and expelling the Parliamentary leaders from the county.

But at that point his success stopped. When he tried to lead the Cornishmen on into Devon they refused to cross the Tamar. They'd been called out, they said, to serve in Cornwall. They would move no farther. It appears over and over again in the Civil War this intense localism of the troops. They will fight in their own counties, for the defence of their homes, but not farther afield. Seeing they were adamant, Hopton yielded. The Cornish levies dispersed, and he set himself to raise a volunteer force that should be willing to serve anywhere.

Meanwhile the Parliament was busy too. That winter they nominated the Earl of Stamford to command their forces in the West. It was a double mistake. Stamford's main asset was that he was a peer and exceedingly wealthy. But he was irritable, cantankerous, self-important; and—just as serious—he was a complete stranger to the West Country. He was a Leicestershire Grey himself, quite unfitted to understand that local western patriotism I have just spoken of. Directly he arrived in Devon he made enemies. He felt strong enough to pursue Hopton's new little army into Cornwall, but in May 1643 he was decisively defeated at the battle of Stratton. It was the first striking military success that either side had won in the West, and it was followed by the rapid advance of Hopton into Devon and Somerset. At Chard he joined up with Hertford and the King's nephew, Prince Maurice; and their combined force continued to march eastward till it met the army of the Parliament, under a commander a great deal more formidable than Stamford, Sir William Waller. There in two battles, at Lansdown just outside Bath and on Roundway Down above Devizes, Waller's army was shattered. The immediate effect was startling. Bristol surrendered to the Royalists—and remember that Bristol was the second city in the kingdom then; the whole of Dorset fell into the King's hands, except Lyme Regis and Poole; a further advance to the east, to London itself, lay open.

The advance did not take place; and once again it was foiled by local provincial feeling. The greatest glory in the fighting had fallen to the Cornishmen, who had scaled the heights at Stratton and again at Lansdown. But their loved and trusted leader, Sir Bevil Grenville, was killed at Lansdown, and that dispirited them—as indeed it dispirited the whole army. And besides, though they had had a great success, sweeping half-way across England, Plymouth was still untaken in their rear, standing between them and their country, a base from which the Parliamentary garrison could —and did—make harrying sorties into Cornwall. They refused to go farther. It was time to get the harvest in and to look to the defence of their own homes.

The stout defence of Plymouth saved the cause of Parliament at this dangerous moment. (In the North, by the way, Hull played just the same part, alarming the Yorkshiremen in the King's army into returning home.) And at the same time another weakness of the Royalists began to appear: the division between their commanders. There were the King's nephews, Rupert and Maurice, dashing professional soldiers, foreigners who cared little for England, only for war in itself; there were their English counterparts, men like Goring and Sir Richard Grenville—Sir Bevil's brother, but utterly unlike him, for Richard was overbearing, selfish and greedy; and there were the moderates, men like Hopton and the Earl of Carnarvon, who looked on the war as a matter of hateful duty and were deeply—almost passionately—concerned to limit its horrors as far as they could. Charles was quite unable to control or to arbitrate between these men, and the parties they formed. His army in the West was never again a single homogeneous unit.

Next summer, in 1644, it was the Parliament that took the offensive, with the Earl of Essex's march into Cornwall. It was a queer move, and very dangerous—an invasion of the most devoted Royalist stronghold in the country. Essex seems to have thought that if he could once control Cornwall the King's party in the West would wither away. But it is also clear that he was worked upon by Lord Robartes and other Cornishmen for their own ends: they were anxious to recover their estates, which the Royalists had seized. Whatever the motives, it was a disastrous attempt. By the middle of August 1644, Essex found himself cooped up between Lostwithiel and the sea, the King's forces closing in on him. There was nothing for it but surrender. The horse, and Essex himself, got away: the rest of the army gave itself up.

Twice, then, the Parliamentarians had attempted the invasion of the West Country, and twice they had been defeated, by the incapacity of their own generals as much as by the Royalists' superiority. The third time it was different. In the spring of 1645 the New Model Army was formed by Parliament. It was a New Model indeed, and new especially in three ways. Its men were drawn from all over England and willing to serve in any part of the country. It was regularly paid: the soldiers received their eightpence a day with exact punctuality. Hence it was a well-disciplined army. Now that was something extremely important at this stage in the war. It was the great weakness of the Royalists that their troops got badly out of hand. Not only were they difficult to control in battle: they took to plundering and living on the country. This in its turn raised the countryside against them, and most of all in the West, where the people, led by substantial farmers and small gentry, formed themselves into bands of Clubmen to protect their property. These Clubmen said they were neutrals in the war: they would defend themselves against plunderers of either party. But by now that had come to mean Royalists only, for in the New Model Army plundering had been virtually stamped out. So it was that in the final western campaign the Parliamentary cause became in a true sense the popular cause, the cause of everybody who valued order, strong government, the quick restoration of peace.

The very first action of the New Model Army took place in the West Country—the relief of Taunton from its second siege in May 1645. Next month the King's cause was broken in the Midlands at Naseby, and the New Model swept down into the West again under Fairfax and Cromwell. It began with a superb, an incredible victory at Langport, and then one by one the Royalist strongholds were reduced: Bridgwater, Bristol, Dartmouth, Exeter and last of all Pendennis castle, gallantly defended by old John Arundell of Trerice until August 1646.

As far as the West was concerned the war was over. Elsewhere in England the struggle went on for two more dreary years, till at last Parliament and army made up their minds to end it by executing the King and setting up a republic. But force led only to counter-force, until in the end the only possible solution was arrived at, painfully and slowly—the restoration of the King with limited power in a civilian, not a military, government. There was the great upshot of the war, a compromise in politics and a corresponding compromise in religion, the bigotries of both sides suppressed.

It was a lesson well understood, even while the war was in progress, by the loftier spirits on both sides. Fairfax, the Parliament's general, had a horror of unnecessary bloodshed. Hopton, one of the noblest

men of his age, had the true cross-bench mind: no
wonder that Chillingworth and Fuller, the apostles of
toleration in the Anglican Church, should both have
chosen to serve as chaplains in his army. Among Hopton's personal friends was Waller, the commander of
the forces opposed to him in the West; and just before
the battle of Lansdown a correspondence passed
between them. In the course of it Waller used these
words: "Certainly my affections to you are so un-
changeable that hostility itself cannot violate my friend-
ship to your person. But I must be true to the cause
wherein I serve. . . . That great God who is the
searcher of my heart knows with what a sad sense I
go upon this service, and with what a perfect hatred
I detest this war without an enemy." There, I think,
is the finest spirit of the seventeenth century—that
resolute loyalty without fanaticism that made the English Revolution in the end a constructive achievement.

X

The Road from the West

by

C. D. BEATTY

We all of us know that England is a very different country to-day from what it was in the seventeenth century, but I wonder if we quite realize how very different it was. "God made the country and man made the town," says the old proverb, but the country that we know is as man-made as the town, and men have been very busy in it for the last three hundred years. I have taken 1663 as the date for my survey, because the civil wars were over, trade was booming, and with the King all England was enjoying its own again. But any other date in that half-century would have done as well.

If we could be taken up in an aeroplane and back in time I don't think that any of us would recognize the greater part of the country we love so much.

In Devon and Cornwall the change wouldn't be quite so great, because that was "old enclosed" country where the patchwork of fields was then, as now, divided by hedges and banks, and bosomed deep in trees; but in the great central plain of England the difference would be startling because that was still largely open —or "champion" as they called it—huge fields anything up to a mile square clustering round the scattered villages, no hedges or fences, just the endless fields of corn, or peas, or beans, blending imperceptibly into each other, with the brighter green of the village meadows here and there, and the duller common pastures of the villages. Big houses and their parks there would be, and of course the great green waves of the downs which not even the twentieth century can wholly tame, and, too, there would be far more trees; but of the farms and fields of to-day there would be no trace, and no trace, too, of the railways driving like sword-cuts through forest and field, through hamlet and town.

I don't think we ever quite realize how much we owe to the railways, bringing us nearly everything we eat and wear and use, taking us away on our holidays or our business trips, and carrying our mails and our newspapers. Three hundred years ago man wanted all those things, too, and yet he had no railways—and of course no aircraft either. How on earth did he manage to live? Well, first of all, of course, he was much more self-sufficient than we are, he grew more of his own food, lived longer in the same place, and moved about far less. But still there were many things he wanted which his own district could not supply, and if he lived in London one of them was clothes, and the hardest wearing cloth was Devonshire kerseys.

I'm going to try in this to trace one of these kerseys from the shop to the wearer, as they say in the advertisements.

The sheep would be largely bred on Exmoor, and on the last Thursday of every October they would be driven down from the moor to stand in a huddled, panting mass in the broad main street at Bampton and find new owners. Their wool was far more valuable than their meat, and the clip of a likely looking flock would soon be the subject of hard bargaining between the graziers and the master clothiers who were by now getting a stranglehold on the cloth industry of the West. Once, not so long ago, "the husbandmen sends his wool to the market which is bought either by the comber or the spinster, and they the next week bring it thither again in yarn which the weaver buys and the market following brings that thither again in cloth, when it is sold either to the clothier or to the merchant, who, after it hath passed the fuller's mill (and sometimes the dryer's vat) transports it". But that is an old story now. In the seventeenth century the clothier was a capitalist on a large scale, and the combers, spinsters and the rest were but jobbing workmen who might or might not own their own homes and spindles, but whose material was supplied by the clothier, and who were paid at piece rates.

Many of these capitalists were very wealthy men

indeed. You can see their monuments in many of our western churches—the Greenway Chapel in St. Peter's, Tiverton, is an outstanding example—and their charities are still valued in almost every town of note in Devonshire. Peter Blundell, who though no scholar was to be the making of more scholars than any other man in the West, is perhaps the best known, but Penrose of Barnstaple, Hurst of Exeter, Watts of Tavistock and dozens of others are hardly less famous.

But we must return to our fleeces!

It would be such a one who bought this clip of ours and whose overseers would be responsible for the numerous processes which would turn it into cloth. We can imagine them easily enough—but the modern foreman would be appalled at the difficulty of their task. For all these processes were carried on not in a large, airy factory, but in cottages scattered over half a county, and every process meant a journey. The overseer would travel on horseback, of course, that we know, but what of the roads on which he jogged his hundreds of miles a month, and how would his precious yarn or cloth be moved from place to place?

First of all we must forget everything we mean when we say a road. West of the Exe wheeled vehicles were unknown and the roads were so narrow that two horsemen would find it difficult to pass. Not much more than half the width of a modern pavement, they would widen like an immense V while the hedges and trees would block the view completely. "An Army might

be marching undiscovered by anybody," says Celia
Fiennes, "for when you are on those heights that show
a vast country about, you cannot see one road." The
surface would approximate to a bad farm track of to-
day. That is to say, there would be some vague foundations of stone and a great deal of mud, particularly
where the road left the hills to drop down to a ford or
just possibly a bridge.

We can still see plenty of these pack-horse tracks by
the way, if we keep our eyes open. Bodmin Moor
above Liskeard is seamed with grass from gullies which
were once the roads trodden by the horses carrying tin
to the sea at Fowey. Exmoor and Dartmoor, too, are
criss-crossed with similar tracks, and only the other day
I saw an unmistakable section of old track near Hol-
combe Rogus—the modern road swung sharply to the
right to avoid a hill, but there, six feet wide between its
hedges, was the old road bravely making for the crest.
Whenever you see a couple of hedges or banks close
together with a similar track between, you can be pretty
sure that you are looking at one of the old roads of
England. Churned by the hooves of innumerable
animals in the valley bottoms, the roads would often
be impassable—it wasn't for nothing that Bunyan made
Christian's road pass through the Slough of Despond—
and it was no one's responsibility to keep them in order.
That is not strictly true, because an Act of 1555 had
made each parish responsible for the upkeep of its own
roads, but the overseer was unpaid and the forced labour

of the parishioners—six days a year all men had to work on the roads or pay the equivalent value in money or materials—was shirked as much as possible. The local J.P.s tried to keep the overseers up to their work with very varying success, and so it is not to be wondered at that the road kept to the hills as much as possible—gradients might be an inconvenience, but valleys meant mud and mud meant "no road this way".

So protected by his "gambadoes"—a special two-sided wooden boot hanging from the saddle instead of stirrups—from the thorns of the hedgerows, the Master Clothier's man would jog from cottage to cottage of his round, examining and paying for the work done and arranging for it to be collected and more raw materials delivered. This collection and delivery would be done by the local carrier who combined in his person the postman, the delivery van and the goods clerk of the day.

Every village had its carrier, and the larger towns had many. Their implement was the pack-horse—a sturdy, specially bred nag not much larger than a modern Exmoor pony. Strapped to its saddle hung large panniers, one on either side, and it was no unusual sight to see a passenger sitting between them. In Devonshire instead of panniers they used two pairs of poles bent like oxbows with their shorter ends resting on the saddle and held together by light cross-pieces between which were piled the load. So between these "crooks" our clip would travel from cottage to cottage varying its form as it went, until finally it was wool no longer but cloth and ready for sale.

Now our Master Clothier has to decide its destination, and much of it will go by sea to the ends of the earth, for everywhere there is a demand for English cloth, from the American plantations to barbaric Muscovy, while the coast-wise trade to London and other English ports is tremendous. So some of our kerseys will go—again by pack-horse—to Exeter, there to be loaded into lighters and towed four miles down the canal to Topsham, where "the ships come up to the bar". For there is a canal now to by-pass Countess Wear—the first of its kind in England allowing small ships and barges to pass right up to Exeter. It wasn't a very good one, and when thirty years later Celia Fiennes saw it she wrote of the bigger and deeper canal that "a man was to accomplish for which they were to give 5 or 6,000 pounds". But still it was a canal with a real lock to control the level of the water, and the forerunner of those hundreds of miles of canal that a century later were to make the Industrial Revolution possible.

At Topsham the ships would be waiting for their cargoes—ships up to one hundred tons and more. They would take passengers too, who would find space as best they might among the cargo and probably spend their voyage in an agony of fear and seasickness in a discomfort greater than we can imagine; but there was no regular packet service from the West Country across the Channel as there was from the ports nearer to London, and, of course, from London itself—the greatest port of all. It was not only by wind and weather that the passengers and cargo were threatened —the Channel swarmed with privateers and pirates; but the freights were comparatively low, and a coaster was not a great prize—so much of our clip would go to London by sea.

Some, however, would certainly go by land. Did not the great Peter Blundell leave money in his will to the carrier who "carried my kersies for me"? So a long string of pack-horses would be loaded up and set off on its journey. By this time the larger carriers were running to schedule from fixed starting-points—though "running" is hardly the right word for a service that averaged twenty-five miles a day. They would leave Exeter on Saturday and arrive the following Friday in London, stay overnight and return the following day or the Monday. So let us go with them on their long journey as they leave the Black Lion in South Street, Exeter, at first light on Saturday morning. At first the string of nine pack-horses—for more were not allowed by law—would be alone, but they would soon be joined by other strings, and with the leaders' bells tinkling merrily they would step out on the great Roman highway that ran straight as an arrow the eighteen miles to Honiton.

This was one of the great trunk roads of the kingdom

—it had been so for fifteen hundred years, and along it even in distant Devonshire could be seen those new-fangled contraptions with wheels. By 1660 it was quite clear that wheels had come to stay, but it was equally clear that the roads could not bear them. In 1622, indeed, carts and wagons with four wheels had been denounced in a Royal Proclamation because they "galled the highways and the very foundations of the bridges". But within twelve years of this Proclamation there were six thousand coaches in London alone, many of them "Hackney Hell Carts" as these earliest of London taxis were called. The Civil Wars had temporarily halted this unparalleled expansion, but by 1658 there was a regular service from Exeter to London by coach, taking four days for the journey which cost £2 (of their money, of course, which we have to multiply by at least ten to get present-day values). For this heavy outlay you would get a seat in a heavy old leather-covered vehicle without any springs, in which the motion was so bad that coach-sickness was a by-word, and there you would stay "from five in the morning till almost nine at night, plunging in the cold and dirt and dark with strange company". Hardly, I think you will agree, an inviting prospect. Still, there was a demand so great that by 1700 there was not a town or important village without its local coach service, and I don't suppose that the earliest railway trains were exactly luxurious nearly two hundred years later. So our pack-horse train would meet one of these monsters on the main highway, and many private coaches, too, near the big towns, just as it would certainly pass some stage wagons—which were just long carts with a canvas tent over them—plodding slowly along with local passengers and local parcels joggled higgledy-piggledy together as they took the villagers to market and back, and occasionally on a longer journey at an average speed of ten to fifteen miles a day.

All this traffic had played havoc with the roads, as you can imagine. Never good at the best of times, they were now collapsing completely under loads they had never been meant to bear. The Government having failed to stop wheeled traffic, had tried to save the roads by forbidding any wheel to have a rim of less than twelve inches broad—in other words to make every coach or wagon into a sort of steam roller, and of course that failed too. But in Hertfordshire in this very year the solution had appeared—there the local justices had been empowered to erect a turnpike and charge a toll of all road users. Thus a fund was created to pay for labour and materials to build roads on good foundations, and it was only a question of time until a durable surface had been found. As the first lock in England at Topsham had already pointed the way to canals, so the first turnpike at Ware in 1663 was to lead in time to coaching roads that were the wonder of the world.

But that was still in the future—at present the riding-horse and the pack-horse carried ninety per cent of the traffic of England on roads little better than tracks. And on these pack-horses which had left the Black Lion Inn at Exeter for the Star in Broad Street, would go at least half of those kerseys for the London trade which had started their life on the backs of hardy little sheep in sight of Dunkery Beacon.

XI

Monmouth's Rebellion

by

PROFESSOR J. SIMMONS

MONMOUTH's rebellion and the Bloody Assizes that followed it are, I suppose, among the most famous episodes in the whole history of the West Country. Other things, much more important, have been quietly forgotten: but the memory of that summer of 1685 has never perished; it is still living, in fact, as I hope to show you later on.

Charles II died in February 1685. Since he left no legitimate children he was succeeded by his brother, the Duke of York: James II. These two brothers present a remarkable contrast. Charles was shrewd and subtle, an adroit manager of men (for he had an accurate eye for all their weaknesses), affable, unprincipled, above all, and always intelligent. James, on the other hand, was both stupid and a fool; not only slow-witted and obstinate, I mean, but wholly without judgment. When he had a choice before him, his instinct infallibly led him wrong. And what made all this worse was that he was honest. He had none of his brother's capacity for dissimulation, for holding back a decision until it was the right moment to announce it. James was ruined in the end, and the cause he stood for, by his fatal combination of faults and untimely virtues.

He was already a declared Roman Catholic: the leader, in Charles II's reign, of the Catholic party in England. To balance him, on the other side, some of the Protestant Whigs had put up as their leader the young Duke of Monmouth, Charles's favourite bastard son. There was a good deal of obscurity about Monmouth's birth; and though Charles himself in 1680, and at other times, plainly asserted he was illegitimate, there was always a possibility of raking up forged documents to prove the contrary. From the Whigs' point of view, at any rate, he was the only possible leader who could be matched against James, Duke of York.

As a man Monmouth had some of the qualities that James so obviously lacked. He was a charming creature, very handsome and winning, easy-tempered and kindly like his father. A good figure-head, in fact, but nothing more: he was a simple light-weight, and when it came to a crisis he lost his head.

When Charles died Monmouth was in the Low Countries. His position was precarious. He knew that his uncle, James II, hated him and would never allow him to return to England: he had nothing to look forward to but a friendless, interminable exile. It is not surprising, with his weak judgment, that he should have listened to the advice of some of the other English *émigrés*, urging him to cross over and turn James off the throne. Directly he had succeeded to the crown— so their story ran—James II had alienated England by his declared Popery. Monmouth had only to land, and the whole country would rise against James. Already the Earl of Argyll was preparing an expedition to land in Scotland. If Monmouth's could be timed to arrive simultaneously in the south of England, James's forces would have to be divided and his chances of successfully defending himself would be gravely weakened. It was a foolish, a feather-headed plan, founded on the fatuous optimism that *émigrés* always show. Monmouth himself seems at first to have been sceptical about the whole business, but gradually his own desperate situation and a little artful persuasion won him over, and he agreed to make the attempt.

From the start it was as nearly hopeless as any such enterprise could be. Monmouth and Argyll did not co-ordinate their plans; both lacked money—but especially Monmouth; there was no certainty whatever that he would get any support in England, nor any credible evidence of James's alleged unpopularity. But once his mind was made up, Monmouth did not turn back. At the end of May he set sail from Holland with three ships and eighty-two men. On 11 June he arrived off Lyme Regis.

It was a well-chosen place. Lyme was famous as a
Puritan town—it had stood a long siege for the Parliament in the Civil War. As a Catholic, James II was
certain to be unpopular there, if anywhere. At the
same time it was a *small* port, small enough to be over-
awed by Monmouth's very small fleet. And at the
outset all went well. The town's officials—the mayor,
the surveyor of the port, and above all the deputy-
searcher of the customs, Mr. Samuel Dassell—were
staunchly loyal to James II's government. But the
town was completely undefended, and while the deputy-
searcher bustled about looking for powder to enable
the guns to be fired, Monmouth and his followers got
ashore. They made their way to the market-place,
where a Declaration was read to the assembled people.
This was a crude manifesto, stuffed with bombast. It
had two main objects: to blacken James II and to assert
Monmouth's legitimacy. It set about the first task with
relish: "We do solemnly declare and proclaim war
against James Duke of York as a murderer and an
assassin of innocent men; a Popish usurper of the
crown; traitor to the nation and tyrant over the people."
More specifically, James was accused, among other
things, of poisoning his brother, the King, and starting
the Great Fire of London. Such charges were not
true, or even very probable. But the Declaration was
designed to make an immediate impression upon
simple-minded people to compel them in large numbers
into Monmouth's army.

It certainly had its effect. Monmouth remained at Lyme four days, in the course of which hundreds of men flocked in from the surrounding country to join him. By 15 June his army may have numbered two thousand. With this force he marched out by the hilly road to the north. His objective was Gloucester, where he hoped to join up with a great army that was being raised for him in Cheshire. On the way he meant to possess himself of Bristol. It was an advantage to the plan that his march would lie through the West Country clothing district, one of the most fervently Protestant parts of England. He might reasonably hope for support here, and above all at Taunton, which had been a bulwark of the Parliamentary cause in the Civil War, only forty years earlier.

He got a good deal of that support. It is this, indeed, that explains the temporary success he enjoyed. If, as it is sometimes thought, his army had consisted solely of deluded rustics armed with pitchforks, it would never have held together as it did. No: the secret of its coherence lies in its stiffening by men of the middle class, Nonconformist tradesmen who believed they were fighting in a cause—the same cause as that of Parliament in the Civil War. They fought out of hatred of Popery and what they believed to be arbitrary government. Look at the names and quality of a few of them among the prisoners tried after the rebellion was over: the clothiers Thomas Whitty of Frome, William Selwood of Chard, Malachi Mallack of Axminster; Michael

Abbott of Honiton, cordwainer; Robert Salt of Upottery, serge weaver. To them one might add Daniel Defoe of London, stocking merchant. We know he was in Monmouth's army, but he was canny enough to avoid capture, though three of his friends were caught and hanged.

As soon as Monmouth had landed, the mayor of Lyme Regis sent off to London to warn the Government. It lost no time. Monmouth was attainted by Act of Parliament, and a price of £5,000 set on his head: all the regular troops in England were ordered to concentrate at Salisbury. The militia of the Western Counties (part police, part Home Guard) had already been called out. But when Monmouth's army came up with them at Axminster, they crumbled away. As one Nonconformist put it, much pleased: "The Lord sent a hornet of fear among them." They had no heart in the King's cause, and many of them took the first chance of going over to join the rebels. With this success behind him, Monmouth pushed quickly on through Chard and Ilminster to Taunton.

There the Declaration was read once again, and then, on Saturday morning, 20 June, Monmouth was proclaimed King in the market-place. It was an empty and ill-advised gesture, for it conflicted with an undertaking, given in the Declaration, that he would leave his title to be determined by Parliament; and it angered some of his followers, who now felt that he was moved by nothing higher than common ambition. This may have been in part the reason why he gained less support than he had hoped for at Taunton. The country-folk continued to stream in, and in mere numbers his army grew mightily; but he was not joined by any gentlemen or substantial tradesmen. Two days later he went on to Bridgwater. Then, turning inland, he made his way to Wells and Shepton Mallet, and so across the Mendips by the main road through Pensford to Keynsham. He was just too late to take Bristol. The King's commander-in-chief, the Earl of Feversham, had arrived there with a small force two days earlier.

It was the crisis of the rebellion, and Monmouth, who was not without common sense, knew it. His enterprise had always been rash. From this point onwards the destruction of his army seemed certain. He fell back on Frome (with a skirmish at Norton St. Philip on the way), and then, remembering his favourable reception in West Somerset, he marched straight back by Shepton to Bridgwater. On their way through Wells, on 1 July, his soldiers did a good deal of damage in the cathedral. They really did stable their horses inside —that is not the libellous story it so often is : a contemporary records it. They also smashed up the organ and stole some silver. No doubt they would have stolen more if they had had the chance, but James Williams the sacrist hid it away.

The army may have got a little out of hand. Yet it held together and put itself into Bridgwater two days later. Throughout its march it had been harassed by the King's troops. They were close in pursuit, and on 5 July Feversham and the whole army advanced to encamp on the plain of Sedgemoor, four or five miles to the south-east of Bridgwater. Monmouth's first thought now seems to have been to make another attempt on Bristol, racing the royal army. But his plan was changed by the discovery of the indiscipline of his opponents. He made up his mind to try and surprise them by a night attack. In Mr. Winston Churchill's words, it was "alike the most daring and the most prudent decision of his life". If he had brought it off, he would have defeated the whole of James II's available forces at one blow.

And he came very near to bringing it off. At eleven o'clock on Sunday night, 5 July—the moon was full —his whole force marched out of Bridgwater. It took a circuitous route, so as to surprise the King's army from an unexpected direction. Twice, on its way, Monmouth's men came near to a party of their enemies: twice they stood motionless while the King's men went by unsuspecting. The whole march was an astonishing feat of discipline in a raw army less than a month old. It brought Monmouth's men to within a mile of their opponents, when they were held up in trying to cross one of the great drains that ran—and still run— across Sedgmoor. Between one and two in the morning the silence was broken by a pistol shot. "Immediately"—I am quoting the words of someone who wrote at the time—"immediately a trooper rides from the place-ward full speed to the camp, calls with all imaginable earnestness twenty times at least 'Beat the drums. The enemy is come. For the Lord's sake beat the drums.'" The King's army started up in the confusion of sleep. The battle had begun.

It was very stubbornly fought through the rest of the night, and for an hour or two into the day. Again one can only marvel at the toughness and constancy of Monmouth's troops, these labourers and farmers and small tradesmen of Somerset and Dorset. They were fighting regulars, and though they had the advantage of numbers they were ill-armed, and such guns as they had never came into play. The battle could have only one end, and by five or six o'clock it was all over, the rebels in flight or hiding in ditches or herded together as prisoners, to be shut up for the next few days wherever it was convenient—in the church at Weston Zoyland, for instance, where fifteen shillings had to be spent afterwards on cleaning the building out, on frankincense and saltpetre and resin to make the air sweet again after the prisoners had left.

Monmouth himself had fled from the battle before it was over. His nerve had completely snapped and he thought only of saving his life. But he was captured near Ringwood in the New Forest, taken to London, and in due course beheaded. He had an easier fate than many of his followers. For them there was nearly two months' waiting in the hot stench of the gaols, and then trial at the Bloody Assizes before Jeffreys, the Lord Chief Justice, and four other judges.

Much nonsense has been written about those Assizes. Some 1,400 rebels were found guilty of high treason and, as the law required, automatically sentenced to death; but less than a seventh of them were actually executed. Of the rest, about 800 were ordered to be transported to the West Indies: the others seem in the end to have got off free. Considering that more than 6,000 men actually bore arms under Monmouth against the King, a total of 200 executions cannot be reckoned a very savage vengeance.

Yet it was a vengeance that James should have forgone. He would have done better to remember the example of Henry VII, who came down into the West after the rising of 1497 and pardoned almost all who were involved in it. James had neither the wisdom nor the magnanimity to do that. As a result, he kindled an undying hatred for himself in the West Country. And his easy triumph over the rebels led him on to his own destruction, until three years later, through plain folly, he lost his throne.

But the thing that interests me most of all about the rebellion and its sequel is the deep mark they made on the memory of West Countrymen. If you go round that countryside now, you will still have the places pointed out to you where Monmouth slept or where rebels were hanged. At Chard, for example, a Hang-Cross Tree stood till 1864: at Stogumber a man who died only fifty years ago remembered being shown as a boy the iron stakes in an old Scotch fir on which the heads of the rebels were stuck. And so on—scores of such tales survive. They may be untrue: many of them are demonstrably absurd. But that is not the point. What is so fascinating about these tales is the proof they afford of the abiding impression the rebellion and the Assizes made upon the people who stood closest to them. Monmouth and Jeffreys have taken their place in the folk-lore of Somerset and Dorset.

XII

Cloth-making in the West
by
G. D. RAMSAY

Aㅣㅌㅎㅇㅜㅎ the reputation of fine West of England cloth is no less high to-day than it was a generation ago, yet perhaps there are not many people who will know that the West Country was once the seat of a widespread cloth manufacture as important in its own day as that of Lancashire or the West Riding is now. Cloth was, of course, made by our prehistoric ancestors and in Roman times, and after the Norman Conquest the woollen fabrics woven in Bristol, Marlborough and other urban centres by the thirteenth century had earned some reputation outside the West Country and even beyond England—later the striped rays of Salisbury were to become specially famous. But it was not until some six hundred years ago, in the fourteenth century, that cloth-making in the West Country made some remarkable strides—for reasons which so far have not been fully explained by historians. All we can say is that large areas of the West Country, outside the greater towns, proved to be extraordinarily suited to the manufacture of cloth, and that a market for it was found not only in England but beyond the seas. The later Middle Ages saw a startling development in the weaving of woollen cloth in and around the villages on the slopes of the southern Cotswolds, from Painswick to Stroud and beyond, and also around the foot of the Mendips from Frome to Wells westwards to Wincanton and in much of north-west Wiltshire from Malmesbury and Devizes to Westbury. Less important areas, where coarser cloth was made, developed in western Somerset and in Devonshire, northwards from Exeter to Tiverton and westwards to Torrington.

We can in part account for this industrial revolution in the West Country—for that is what it was—by geological and geographical factors. In the areas where cloth-making took root on a large scale there was generally a supply of fullers' earth close at hand, and also water-power for driving the fulling-mills in which the cloths were thickened and lost their grain. There was, too, sufficient food available in the neighbourhood to support a manufacturing population—indeed, the connection between the West Country woollen industry and agriculture was very close, as will be seen. The presence close at hand of fine Cotswold and other wool may have been important at first, but was less so later, for even before the end of the Middle Ages wool and yarn were being sent to the looms of the south-west from the Midlands and even farther afield. Still less important was the influence of foreign immigrants, who do not appear to have contributed in any notable way to the progress of the West Country woollen industry. It developed, when all is said and done, because its products were well made and well liked. The time of most rapid expansion came in the early sixteenth century, when the financial policy of Henry VIII gave more than a touch of inflation to the national economy and a consequent fillip to industry; in his reign we know that the exports of broadcloth, much, if not most, of which came from the West Country, almost doubled.

We have a very interesting picture of the West of England in these years from the pen of John Leland, an antiquary and topographer who travelled on horseback in the fifteen-thirties all over the country, and whose jottings at every turn disclose to us the significance of cloth-making in the West. Bath, he tells us, "hath been of a long time since most maintained by making of cloth", though owing to the death of three large employers it had somewhat decayed. Riding on through Paulton and Chewton Mendip he noticed the city of Wells "to be large and for the most part built of stone". The streets, he says, "have streamlets of springs almost in every one running" and the town "occupieth making of cloth". Similarly in Gloucestershire he found, for instance, Wotton-under-Edge to be a pretty market town, "well occupied with clothmakers, having one fair long street and houses well builded in it"; from there he rode a mile or two to Dursley, which he describes as "a pretty clothmaking town", and on to Tortworth, where he tells us "there be some good clothmakers". And thus he describes many another village where the weaver's loom is now a thing unknown.

The woollen industry which Leland observed to be so widespread in the West Country some four hundred years ago was organized on what economic historians call the domestic system, a very elastic term. Wool was spun by women in houses and cottages all over the countryside; sometimes it was imported into the West Country already in the form of yarn. It was to some extent bought by small craftsmen, but generally it came to belong to large capitalist employers, known as clothiers, who delivered it out to the weavers to make the cloth on the looms they kept in their own homes. The finishing processes of fulling, dyeing, shearing and so forth were then completed in a more centralized way under the eye of the clothier when the cloth had been returned to him by the weaver. It was then up to the clothier to take or send the cloth to the market, which even for Devonshire generally in the sixteenth century meant London. There it was mostly bought by the great exporting merchants to be shipped overseas.

We must be careful not to let any sort of idyllic

picture of happy weavers and kindly clothiers living in harmony in Tudor times to form in our minds: work was hard and long, weavers and clothiers all too often found themselves plunged into debt, the standard of life was low and there were weeks of crisis when the harvest was poor and men rioted for bread. But to a large extent cloth-making, particularly outside the towns, was in those days a part-time occupation; the women did the spinning when they could, and their men turned to the loom when there was no pressing work in the field to be done. Even the clothier was often a considerable farmer. A good example of the well-to-do weaver who also did some farming is provided by Thomas Wydon of Tellisford, near Wells, who died in 1554, and in his will left behind him, for division among his wife and their three sons and four daughters, no less than three looms; he also left a couple of sheep to each of his children, and mentions others, so that he must have kept at least a small flock, and since to his third son he bequeathed an acre of wheat "at the bush in the field", we may assume that he was in some very modest way a farmer.

When trade was brisk, as in the reign of Henry VIII, some clothiers made their fortunes, and their sons were able to retire gracefully from business and found county families. Near many a West Country village there is to be found a pleasant Tudor manor-house, such as that at Great Chalfield in Wiltshire, which was built by a successful clothier anxious to set up as a country gentleman; there are also fine old houses at Bradford-on-Avon and many other places still standing to testify to the wealth accruing to the cloth-making capitalist three or four centuries ago. The London merchant, who also sometimes made a fortune from dealing in and exporting West Country cloth, has likewise left traces of his wealth; for instance, two colleges at Oxford still flourishing to-day, Trinity and St. John's, were founded in the middle of the sixteenth century by merchants who probably earned much of their riches by exporting cloth made in Somerset, Gloucester and Wiltshire.

It may be wondered what markets abroad there were so thronged with buyers of West Country cloth. In the sixteenth century there was a sale for the cloths of Devonshire and Somerset in Spain, Portugal and western France; we know that at Bilbao in Spain, for example, there was a welcome for cloths made from Isle of Wight wool at Shepton Mallet. These were done up, after the fashion of the time, in packs of ten, two of which had to be plain blue, two azure, two light sky colour, two light violet and two of what were described as "light popinjay green". The scarlet cloths for which Stroud in Gloucestershire became famous—the celebrated "Stroudwater scarlets"—found a wide market in various parts of Europe, and, incidentally, in a later generation supplied the red coats in which the armies of Marlborough fought. But in Tudor times the

main product of West Country looms was fine broadcloth. This, while still undyed, was despatched to
London by pack-horse and was then exported, mainly
for consumption in central Europe. It was the increasing demand for fine English broadcloth in the fifteenth
and early sixteenth centuries to clothe the noblemen
and city fathers of Germany that in the main provoked
the great expansion of cloth-making in the West
Country.

This trade had its ups and downs, but while it lasted
it was a good trade and it brought prosperity to the
West of England. Until the middle of the sixteenth
century it was almost continuously on the upgrade.
But then there began serious political and religious dis-
turbances, both in Germany and the Netherlands, and
these caused much dislocation and distress to the cloth-
makers of the West of England. It was later the great
Continental upheaval known as the Thirty Years War
that fatally diminished the German market for the
West Country and compelled its cloth-makers and their
London exporters more urgently to look to new
methods and new purchasers if they were to survive.
The seventeenth century was indeed an age of slump
and experiment for the West Country woollen industry.
The merchants first of Exeter and then of Bristol began
seriously to threaten practical monopoly of the London exporters, and all sorts of new varieties of cloth,
including serges and other types of worsted, began to
be made. Not without much hardship the industry

struggled to its feet again, with new markets in the Mediterranean and Levant, in the Baltic and across the Atlantic, which were largely secured by our political and naval triumphs over first the Dutch and then the French in a series of hard-fought wars known to every schoolboy.

And so in the eighteenth century the industry enjoyed another period of expansion, though these years were increasingly marked by friction between employers and employees. Large capitalists now dominated the making of West Country cloth, and both parties to industrial disputes were well organized; a famous episode occurred in 1756, when the weavers of Gloucestershire compelled the government to intervene to maintain—temporarily—their wages. Technical developments soon intensified these outbursts; when in 1776 the spinning-jenny was first introduced into the West Country at Shepton Mallet there were considerable riots, the prelude to a troubled period. In the early nineteenth century Trowbridge was a storm-centre, and industrial action there was concerted by the local labour leaders with the Luddites of Yorkshire. The social distress that followed the persistent application of new technical devices varied from place to place, but much increased when from 1816 or 1817 onwards the use of steam power in the woollen manufacture led to the gradual and painful transference of the greater part of the industry to the North Country. However, the West Country woollen industry in the twentieth century, although no longer one of the larger industries of the kingdom, is more than holding its ground, and its products, with their established reputation, are among those for which a readiest export market is found.

XIII

Bristol and the Slave Trade

by

PROFESSOR C. M. MACINNES

In 1553 three Bristol ships, laden with cloth, jet and amber, sailed for Morocco; so began the long association of this port with the African trade. Gold, ivory and forest products were the principal commodities sought for at first, for, although some slaves were carried by Englishmen to the new world in the later sixteenth and early seventeenth centuries, it was not till after the Restoration that the trade in negroes was taken seriously in hand. For many years London fought hard to retain her monopoly of this traffic, but she was compelled at last to recognize the claims of the out-ports. But long before this occurred, the Bristol slave trade was firmly established, and well before the close of the seventeenth century it had become one of the principal sources of the city's prosperity. This trade continued to expand during the first half of the eighteenth century, and in 1753 Bristol sent twice as

many ships to Guinea as London, but by that time
Liverpool had taken the lead.

Eighteen years later Bristol with her 23 ships came
third, as against London's 58 and Liverpool's 107. Thereafter the decline of Bristol was rapid, and indeed, before
the close of the century, she was already preening herself
on her superior virtue, since, unlike the wicked city of
Liverpool, her humane and benevolent merchants took
no share in this melancholy traffic. It may be said in
passing, however, that they continued to make full use
on their plantations of the Africans with which their
successful rivals supplied them.

While, then, the slave trade was for over a century
the chief concern of her merchants, Bristol was never
for any considerable length of time the principal British
slave port. In the course of the eighteenth century,
mayors and sheriffs of Bristol, aldermen, city councillors, masters and members of the Society of Merchant Venturers, Members of Parliament for the city—
all of these shared in the trade. These distinguished
citizens of the past were not wicked and cruel men,
but pillars of society in their own time, and there seems
to be little justification for that macabre self-satisfac-
tion which some Bristolians appear to derive from
recollections of the presumed depravity of their for-
bears. If they are to be judged, then they should be
judged by the standards of the time in which they lived,
and since the nation as a whole applauded their enterprise there would appear to be no special reason why

they should be singled out for particular condemnation.

In Bristol the trade was usually conducted by small or moderately sized firms of two or six partners or more. The vessels employed were of many rigs—ships, brigs, brigantines, snows, galleys and schooners all appear in the records—but the most surprising thing about them was their diminutive size.

Thus in seventy ships examined which were engaged in carrying slaves from Africa to Virginia, the tonnage ranged from 50 to 250 tons burden, but the majority were in the group 76 to 100 tons. A 50-tonner carried an average of 190 negroes. For those whose tonnage was between 51 and 75, the average cargo was 166, and 233 for the group 76 to 100 tons. The *Greyhound* of 120 tons carried 410 Africans, and the *Hector* of 200 tons, 512. Twenty-eight of these seventy vessels were built in Bristol, seven in other parts of the kingdom, twenty-five in the plantations and ten were prizes. At the time of the registration in Bristol their average age was ten years. Several were over twenty years of age, and one was twenty-nine, which appears to suggest that ships were commonly diverted to the slave trade when their best days were passed. Slave ships were often barricaded on poop and forecastle, and the guns that peeped through at convenient places to cover the waist of the vessel where the negroes came up for air and exercise were grim reminders of the nature of the trade.

So much for the ships, and now what of the men

who sailed in them? The slave trade was never popular among sailors, but this repugnance was due, not so much to the nature of the trade, as to the evil reputation of the West Coast—"beware and take care of the Gulf of Benin, there is one comes out for forty goes in"—admirably expressed the sailor's point of view. Death and desertion were indeed commonplace occurrences on these voyages; thus out of 940 men that made up the crews of 24 Bristol slavers in 1787, 216 died during the voyage, 239 deserted or were discharged in the plantations, 10 out of 56 completed the voyage in one vessel, and 14 out of 44 in another. But these losses were probably above the average. Slave ships normally carried larger crews than other merchantmen, but usually the proportion of able-bodied seamen was less.

What, then, did their cargo consist of?—cloth of various kinds, muskets, pistols, powder and shot, beads, metal bars, trinkets of different sorts, spirits, a medicine chest, slave provisions, cooking utensils, and a grim assortment of handcuffs, chains, shackles, collars, branding-irons and whips.

With luck a merchant might expect to make three profits on a voyage. The cargoes taken out from Bristol were exchanged for slaves at a profit; the slaves were disposed of at a profit in the plantations, and the colonial produce brought home was sold at a profit.

It was always a hazardous trade, however, and a voyage might well turn out a total loss. As England was frequently at war during the eighteenth century, enemy ships of war were to be reckoned with, while both at peace and at war pirates were a continual source of anxiety. When a ship arrived safely on the coast the captain's worries were not over. Indeed they were just beginning. There, Portuguese, Frenchmen, Dutchmen, Germans, Danes, Swedes, Englishmen and Colonials competed with each other for slaves. They caroused, they fought, they cheated each other, they broke every law of God and man in their mad rush to collect the negroes and be off.

The ships of the Royal African Company, or those that acknowledged its rights, resorted to the Companies' forts, where they found slaves already collected and ready to be put aboard.

Sometimes slaves were procured in a market, controlled by a local chief or trader. Bristol firms frequently sent their agents in advance to buy negroes in order that the ship should not be kept too long on the coast.

If the local supply was insufficient, boats were sent up-river to trade. Villages were attacked at the dead of night, and all the able bodied were carried off. Sometimes the slavers waited like beasts of prey for the conclusion of a war which they had fomented in order to enslave the conquered, and if there were not enough of these, the conquerors as well.

According to one writer, Bristol captains placed triple irons on those that were sturdy and "kept their own men sober and on a barricaded quarter deck". During the dismal middle passage, as the voyage from Africa to the plantations was called, because it was the middle section in the triangular trade between England, Africa and the plantations, the sufferings of the slaves were indescribable. Many of them were terrified at the sight of the ocean which they had never seen before, and the violent movement of these strange floating prisons in which they were confined brought on seasickness and intensified their dread. It was commonly believed among them that their captors intended to kill and eat them, and so, when opportunity offered, many a fear-maddened wretch threw himself overboard to escape his tormentors. While some captains tried honestly to mitigate the sad lot of their victims as much as they were able, brutality prevailed on the average slaver, for captains and crews like the negroes were a prey to fear. Every sailor had heard terrible stories of slave mutinies at sea, and so they were constantly on watch for the first sign of insubordination. This they punished with fiendish brutality. Mutinies were rare, however; but the fear of epidemics was never absent on the middle passage, and references to losses of 60 to 100 or more slaves on a single voyage recur in the documents.

Even when the slave ship arrived in the plantations, the troubles of the captain were still not at an end. Colonial legislators had an unpleasant habit of placing special import duties on slaves, as many a petition to Parliament from irate merchants in London, Bristol and Liverpool testifies; or again, the Colonial market might be overstocked when the ship arrived in port, or the cargo might for some other reason be unsaleable; slaves, after all, were just a commodity like any other, though it is true that as each slave was valuable the owners never tired of pressing their captains to see that the Africans were landed in good condition.

There is a great deal in the correspondence of the factors with their principals about long and short credits, brokerage charges, market conditions, but the feelings of the slaves were never considered—they were merely so many cattle, horses or sheep.

Sometimes a captain might sell a whole cargo at the first port of call, but at others it was necessary to peddle them round the plantations from Barbados to Virginia before they were all sold. A captain, in desperation, might sell them to middle men, called "soul drivers", who herded them about the colony from estate to estate till all were disposed of. As a last resort the miserable dregs of a cargo might be got rid of by the "scramble". When this happened the ship was darkened with sails, the men were placed at the main-deck and the women at the quarter-deck. When the signal was given the would-be purchasers rushed through the barricaded door into the interior blackness with the ferocity of beasts in order to encircle as many as they could with the ropes they carried.

When put up for sale in the markets ashore, the slaves were brought in one at a time and mounted upon a stand before the bidders who handled and inspected them with as little concern as if they had been examining cattle at Smithfield.

What, it may be asked, did slaves cost in Africa, and how much did they fetch in the plantations? These questions are not easy to answer, since the price of a slave varied according to age, sex, physical condition, place of origin, scarcity or plenty, intensity of demand and so on. Again, the most common medium of exchange on the coast was a bar of iron, but the value of this fluctuated from place to place and from decade to decade.

In the early eighteenth century on the Gold Coast slaves were to be had at from £11 to £14 apiece. They might be sold in the Colonies at between £20 and £30. Between 1660 and 1807 once the trade was abolished there was a perceptible rise in the price level, and so at the close of the eighteenth century a freshly landed, healthy young slave would sell in Jamaica for £50.

This, then, was the brutal trade against which the conscience of England revolted in the closing years of the eighteenth century, and which Wilberforce made it his life's work to destroy.

XIV

The Culture of Eighteenth-Century Bath
by
JOHN SUMMERSON

I WANT to describe Bath in this talk not so much as
a place as an *event*—as a phenomenon in time, something which happened. To do this I am going to ask
you to stand back from the historical map and to look
for a moment not at Bath but at England—England in
the reign of Charles II. There we see a country whose
life was still essentially rural, a country whose wealth
was the land, whose governors were the hereditary pos-
sessors of land, a country whose life beat most strongly
in the individual parish, the manor-house, the parson-
age, the farm.

It was a rough, hearty, half-Gothic England, where
there was little to choose between the manners of the
squire and those of his yeoman neighbour; nor was
there much more polish or refinement to be found
among the merchants in the towns. But over it all,
very, very thinly spread, was another kind of life

altogether—that issuing from Charles's Court at White-hall. This was a cosmopolitan, leisured, elaborate life, not without its vices, but neither stupid nor intolerant of better things in its pursuit of the one grand objective—systematic and continuous amusement.

Now the phenomenon of Bath really begins with this pursuit—this quest of pleasure by that section of society which took its bearings from Whitehall. The court was held at Whitehall during the winter months. In the spring it moved and went, with the King, to one or other of his country palaces. The circles around the court broke up; the noblemen and gentry of whom they consisted packed off home to their country seats and became agriculturally minded till near the end of the year.

This long summer break in the round of social intercourse in London did not, of course, suit everybody. To the most active pleasure-seekers it was a bore to have to go and sit in the country, where the only company was that of squires, parsons and farmers to whom the conventions and delights of Whitehall were something totally foreign. So they began to cast about for alternatives. And Bath was one of them.

Bath then was a small centre of woollen manufacture, not by any means easily accessible and with no social attractions whatever. It had one peculiar feature—the warm springs—which were supposed to be good for certain complaints. Sterility in women was one of them, and it was the magic of that possibility that brought

Queen Catherine of Braganza to Bath, with the King and his court, in 1663; while about the same time the King's physician decided that Bath offered greater therapeutic advantages than some of the foreign spas which his patients had been frequenting.

Bath, therefore, from 1663, enjoyed its first boom as a health resort. But what is so very curious in its history is that, almost immediately, it became a centre not merely for health-seeking but for pleasure-seeking, a resort of all those people who were casting about for some way of bridging the intervals between the London seasons. The reason is, I suppose, that the Bath invalids, being people of rank, automatically made a focus of patrician life, a sub-centre of Whitehall, and from that sub-centre the really astonishing phenomenon of eighteenth-century Bath, the pleasure-metropolis of Great Britain.

I have gone into the beginnings of the phenomenon in some detail, because we are apt to take Bath for granted, to think "well, of course, the waters made Bath", and leave it at that. There was far more to it. The fact is that late seventeenth-century England was looking for a playground, and for various reasons, of which the waters were one, Bath was chosen. It might very easily have been Tunbridge Wells: it might have been Epsom or Newmarket. But although both these places had their successes, it was Bath which swept the board.

Life at Bath in the early days of its great period

must, I think, have been rather like life on an ocean liner. The comparison may sound absurd, but what I mean is this: Here were a number of people come together in a small place with one ostensible object (arrival in the case of the liner, cure in the case of Bath) with nothing to do but to pass the time and amuse themselves. We all know or can visualize life on a liner: the escaping crooks, the card-sharpers and confidence tricksters who seize their opportunities; and every Atlantic trip has its flirtations, its gossip and its little scandals, or sometimes its quite big scandals. All those things, pleasant and unpleasant, which a life of idleness breeds, bred at Bath. And just as, on a liner, a certain degree of punctuality and discipline is required of the passengers, and a certain amount of organized entertainment laid on, so in early eighteenth-century Bath somebody had to keep things going and to keep them—more or less—straight. There was no reason why that somebody should have materialized. But the fact is that he did. His name was Richard Nash.

"Beau" Nash was certainly one of the main factors in the success of the Bath phenomenon. He was a playboy, of no particular ability but with one tiny streak of genius, the genius to make a party go. He was given the mock-pompous rôle of "king of Bath" (there had, by the way, been such a character in Bath for centuries), and he ruled the place with a rod which everybody delightedly accepted as a rod of iron (again I am reminded of the serio-comic rule of King Neptune when a liner crosses the Equator). Under Nash, the life of Bath began to go with a swing, at the pace and rhythm he dictated.

And there were other characters, less conspicuous, less flamboyant than Nash, but no less important to the success of the phenomenon. The name of Dr. Oliver, for instance, is not likely to be forgotten so long as the kind of biscuit he invented or approved retains the name of "Bath Oliver". And even without the biscuit, the Doctor's work at the Bath Hospital and his valiant championship of the waters deserves all honour.

Oliver was a Cornishman; he came from Ludgvan. He was one of two great Cornishmen, born within a year of each other, to whom Bath owes much. The other was Ralph Allen, and his story is remarkable indeed.

He was the son of the man who kept the Duke William at St. Blazey. As a lad he got a job in a local post office and was eventually promoted to the office at Bath. There he distinguished himself by a piece of secret service work, which drew the favourable attention of General Wade, whose natural daughter he eventually married. He was a born organizer, a promoter, one of those people who see just half an inch ahead of what others see and by that half-inch become indispensable to society. He knew (what everybody knew) that a postal system which obliged a letter from an addressor in Bath to an addressee in Worcester to go round by

London was monstrously inefficient. He saw the value of cross-posts *and* (here comes the extra half-inch) he saw how to make them work—and pay. Devising the system himself and farming it himself, he earned, without the slightest apparent trouble, an income of £12,000 a year (say £40,000 a year, tax free, in our money) for the rest of his long life.

What has all this to do with Bath? Only this: that it endowed the city with a great, permanently resident, patronal figure, a solid, genial character, a man universally interested in everything to do with the city—from the building of its hospitals (St. Oliver's Hospital) to the exploitation of its stone quarries. Allen became "the man of Bath". He built himself the gorgeous classical palace of Prior Park and there entertained the better elements—the bishops, poets, men of letters, even sometimes the royal family—among Bath's visitors. He was the wise and virtuous foil to the giddy, tinsel-figure of Beau Nash. His modesty has, thanks to Pope, passed into a byword; for it was of him that Pope wrote:

Let humble Allen with an awkward shame
Do good by stealth and blush to find it fame.

How often we use those last five words! But how many of us remember the name of the man who was the cause of their being written? Yet Ralph Allen, the Cornish publican's son, was one of the great figures of his time, one of the great personalities of the Bath phenomenon.

But to return to the city itself. We must not imagine that in the early days of Nash, of Oliver and Allen, Bath was anything like the size or had anything like the appearance of the city of to-day. It was still, in the first quarter of the eighteenth century, only the size of a small market town, a cluster of narrow streets in the bend of the Avon, dominated by the tower of the abbey. The existence of the Roman Bath was unsuspected, and the baths which were used were squalid, inconvenient and at times disorderly. There were no hotels in the modern sense, and lodgings were plain even when they were not dirty. Probably the very discomfort of Bath enabled Nash to organize his "passengers". Private entertaining being difficult in the circumstances, it was accepted as unfashionable. Nash's programme was a public programme; everybody followed it and mixed with all comers, whatever their rank. Therein, perhaps, was the greatest attraction which Bath had to offer. The duke and the upstart, the countess and the provincial débutante, the bishop and the crook all mixed in this holiday atmosphere, accepting but one rule, the rule of Nash.

Old Bath was too small, too old and shabby a vessel to contain this life for long, and inevitably the moment came when the city had to expand. Just as Nash had, as if by a miracle, appeared on the scene at the instant when Bath required discipline, just as Oliver had come to give medical repute, and Allen to provide a background of solid benevolence, so another genius, John

Wood, materialized, when she required buildings. Wood was a most interesting person. He combined a thorough, practical knowledge of building technique and finance with a romantic passion for classical archaeology—a combination which could only have occurred, I think, in eighteenth-century England. Wood had never been to Rome, but he was bent on re-establishing Bath as a Roman city. He wanted to build a Forum, a Colosseum and what he called a Gymnasium—somewhat inappropriate projects, you may think, for a provincial spa, but the fact is that he did succeed in building the first two.

His Forum is represented by South Parade and the open space adjoining it; his Colosseum is, of course, the Circus—an inside-out version of it, absurdly smaller and consisting simply of thirty odd houses and no arena at all; but still a fair visual equivalent of the great Roman monument. It is hardly necessary to add that Wood was the architect employed by Allen to build Prior Park.

So there were the rigid components of the Bath phenomenon—the social and medical discipline and the geometrical plans and elevations. The life within that framework came from all England. English society gathered in Bath as at a court or a metropolis—and the essence of the whole thing is that Bath was neither of these, neither a court nor a metropolis, but simply— Bath. That is why I have called it a phenomenon. It was a creation of pure social instinct guided by all sorts of fortuitous circumstances whose interaction it is impossible wholly to analyse or explain.

The history of Bath in the eighteenth century is, in effect, the cultural history of England during that period. The city was a limb of London, the summer capital, the pleasure capital. In art, literature, politics, manners, even religion, Bath played an equal part with London. What she took from London she gave back in full measure. It was at Bath, for instance, that at the behest of Nash, gentlemen first began to leave off wearing swords: when they returned to London they did not resume them. Much of the mildness which characterized English society in the latter half of the eighteenth century was due to the softening discipline of Bath. Again, John Wood, who brought to Bath the hard formalities of London architecture, left behind him a style of town-planning which is reflected in London's Regent Street and Regent's Park as well as in the new town of Edinburgh and a dozen other fine cities. In religion it was at Bath that people of the wealthier classes first lent an ear to the stern sincerities of Wesley's methodism, and I wonder how much in the way of tolerance and mutual understanding England owes to that.

As for literature and painting, the influence of Bath is simply incalculable. Here the writer could see right inside the mechanism of social man; here was the material for romance and satire all ready to his hand. Here the painter found his sitter, his patron and his public, the singer his most eager listeners, the actor and the playwright one of the most critical and stimulating audiences in Europe.

The Bath phenomenon came to an end with the golden century with which it will always be associated. In Jane Austen's time the public life at Bath, diluted to excess, like a party with too many guests, had already become impersonal and unmanageable. People were entertaining each other London-fashion, and no longer playing the social game according to the public rules. The game, indeed, was played out. Bath had had its day. England was a different place, and although the city continued to prosper as a great health resort, the Bath phenomenon—that entrancing, beautiful, scandalous cruise across the eighteenth century—was finished for ever.

XV

Cobbett Rides West

by

GEOFFREY GRIGSON

WILLIAM COBBETT was a busybody. He was a politician, a political journalist, and a farmer, plain but by no means simple, insufferably determined, immensely opinionated, frequently wrong in his opinion, unquenchably curious, firm in his belief that large cities were detestable and mainly inhabited by drones, and that the primary welfare of England depended upon the land and those who worked the land. After all, farming is still, even in 1949, the largest of all our industries, employing the most numerous single body of men; and farming in the eighteen-twenties, when Cobbett began his rural riding, was severely hit by a multiplicity of causes.

So this egoistic democrat, who was himself the child of a small Hampshire farmer, and who always remembered the days when he had worn a smock-frock and carried a wooden bottle, like a shepherd's boy on the

145   K

downs, rode west and rode round and round about, to see, if he could, the condition of the farms, the farmers, the farm workers, the parsons and the landlords, in all the counties of England. Things were wrong.

Cobbett had his own somewhat peculiar ideas of why things were wrong. His energy and temperament compelled him to collect, or complete, the evidence for his ideas. So upon horseback, in all weathers, when he was over fifty, he began his celebrated rides. In the West, the county of which he recorded most was Wiltshire; and as I live in Wiltshire, I shall consider for the most part Cobbett's Wiltshire evidence.

Agriculture in the world is about ten thousand years old; and by no means so old as that in the British Isles; and when Cobbett rode up and down, agriculture was over the crest from its older and cruder phases into its modern shape. I live myself in a village in North Wiltshire, surrounded by cold and deep land which was a forest of oaks until well into historic times. A few descendants of those oak trees are scattered about in the fields. Clearances of the forest can hardly have begun until after the Saxon invasions, so that agriculture in my parish is not even two thousand years old. The divisions of the land, the boundaries of the farms, the utilization of the soil, are still affected by the Saxon revolution in farming and by the feudal system into which it changed.

When Cobbett arrived, my own parish was only, in those very years, by an enclosure act, discarding the remnants of the old feudal system. The old open fields worked in common by farmers whose houses, buildings and yards were grouped together in the village, were at last split up and enclosed into individual farms. The water-logged land was not suitable for corn, and was dangerous for sheep in the winter months. Enclosure made it possible to drain the land and turn it into pasture for cattle and milk; and pasture it remains even now.

But just as some of the old oaks of the forest, the primeval forest, or at least their descendants, still remain in these pastures, so, in our village, our lives are still affected by remnants of the feudal system. The open fields were enclosed—yes, but the landlord and the farmers could not be expected to pull down their houses and buildings and build new ones conveniently near the land apportioned to each new farm. So the old grouping of the farmsteads persists, inconveniently to this day: four sets of houses, yards, and outhouses are all grouped together within a hundred yards of each other.

The farming, then, which Cobbett investigated and described a hundred and twenty years ago, was rooted in conditions of a past which still was not dead, which still has not died even in 1949, and which, in one sense, can never die. History studies the complex, the divided and sub-divided roots of the present, and the roots are a living past. One thing merges into another, and condition provokes another condition, *ad infinitum*. Thus when Cobbett entered Wiltshire in November 1821, when agriculture was deep in a transient depression which added itself to all the modifying historical influences upon the countryside, he remarked, as he was to remark so often in his rides, upon the miserable poverty of the farm workers he saw, not so far away from my village.

He was riding from Hurstbourn Tarrant in Hampshire to Marlborough. "The labourers along here," he wrote, "seem very poor indeed. Farm houses with twenty ricks round each, besides those standing in the fields; pieces of wheat, 50, 60 or 100 acres in a piece; but a group of women labourers . . . presented such an assemblage of rags as I never saw before even amongst the hoppers at Farnham, many of whom are common beggars. I never before saw *country* people, and reapers, too, looking so miserable in appearance as these. There were some very pretty girls, but ragged as colts and pale as ashes. The day was cold, too, and frost hardly off the ground; and their blue arms and lips would have made any heart ache but that of a seat-seller or a loan-jobber."

Here, too, was a condition, a condition of poverty, which provoked a counter-condition. The steps could be traced between these miserable, ragged men and women and children, between their misery in a transient depression and all the legislative and social steps which have put shoes on the feet of the children, given them schools and school meals, and given their fathers a living wage, and taken themselves and their mothers off the land.

I have twice spoken of a transient depression in agriculture at the time of Cobbett's "Rural Rides". What was the depression? What was its nature and how was it caused? From the "Rural Rides" themselves, and from Cobbett's forcible but muddled views, his exclamations and his anger and his vituperation, it would not be so easy to give an answer. Cobbett's own reasoning is not much more reasonable than a farm worker's song which was current in Wiltshire and perhaps in Hampshire as well round about this time. The song declared that the farm workers were "pinched in their bellies and pinched in their clothes".

Here's first to those farmers who do sell the corn
And they are all as big rogues as ever were born;
They are never contented, but still they have none,
If the land were to yield fifty bushels for one;

and then in five more stanzas it goes through a list of rogues who should all swing together on the gallows, the mean landlord, the thieving miller, the cheating butcher, and the cheating baker who mixes bean flour and alum into the loaves. Cobbett's list of rogues and reasons is a bit more sophisticated, but not—altogether —more convincing.

The drones. The drones who eat the corn and eat the taxes. The drones especially in the big cities, and especially in the Wen, as he always names it, of London. Cobbett's drones included politicians who sat for rotten boroughs such as Wootton Bassett, or Old Sarum, or Calne, or Westbury, place-holders and middle-men such as the Quaker dealers in corn, sinecurists, pensioners and parsons, creatures, wrote Cobbett, when he got to Wylye, "that have an inheritance in the public carcase, like the maggots that some people have in their skins". The remark was prompted by a non-resident rector of Wylye, who had a living elsewhere in Hampshire. Cobbett hated these pluralist clergymen who used tithe, a tax upon the land, to breed families of corn-devouring idlers, where tithe, he maintained, had originally been granted to unmarried parsons for their living and for distribution among the poor, and not as a "premium for breeding". But the worst rogue of all to Cobbett was the new kind of landlord, industrialists and financiers turned squire—turned into merciless squires—"Squires of Change Alley", who had built up their big estates from the smaller holdings of yeomen and the lesser gentry who had been ruined by the changes in agriculture in the preceding fifty years.

What Cobbett did not see—or did not see clearly—was the complicated nature of these agricultural changes and the depression. The high prices which farm produce had commanded in the French wars had collapsed after 1815. Farmers had to retrench, and retrenched at the cost of labour. That was one cause. But the deeper cause was this revolution in agriculture.

Enclosures in Wiltshire alone had transformed the rural economy in Cobbett's lifetime. Small farmers became farm-labourers, farm-labourers lost their rights in the waste land of the manors, on which they could pasture geese and a cow and get their firing. Industry was also being transformed and collected into the factories, so that the Wiltshire farm-worker's families no longer could eke out their living, for example, by spinning wool at home. The war raised the cost of living, and the post-war depression broke upon a countryside which had not had time to readjust itself to a new world.

Farming was changing from subsistence-farming to capitalized farming to feed the new proletariat of the cities created by industrialist capital. The farm-worker who had boarded with the farmers and lived off the produce of the land which he worked, now had to live on his own and live (in a reign of high prices) on a wage. He had to buy—the writer of that song was right—for the first time from the butcher and the baker and the brewer.

Yet these rogues of his imagination were not the causes of his distress, but parallel symptoms of that distress. Cobbett was too much inclined to take symptoms for causes. The husband of 1949 looks at his dinner and says, "Starch again." The wife replies, "Go and see Mr. Strachey."

Cobbett, with the same near-sightedness of a contemporary, blamed (though they were not free of blame) his squires of Change Alley, the politicians, the parsons, the corn-dealers, and so on. The canals at Devizes, he remarked, was "the great channel through which the produce of the country is carried away to be devoured by the idlers, the thieves and the prostitutes who are all tax-eaters, in the Wens of Bath and London". He maintained that the corn only went to his "tax-eaters". If Wiltshire corn was exchanged between two sets of workers, industrial and agricultural, if a wagon-load of wheat went off from the Vale of Pewsey in the morning, and came back in the evening loaded with the produce of industry, instead of coming back more or less empty, as it did, then the Wiltshire people might see it go off without tears in their eyes.

Cobbett was too near events on his "Rural Rides"— and too bigoted—to see the complexity of their causes, so you must read his famous book cautiously. None the less Cobbett's picture of the poverty, misery and depopulation in Wiltshire and in Hampshire and elsewhere in the eighteen-twenties is in itself true, moving and brilliantly recorded.

XVI

The Industrial Revolution in Cornwall

by

F. L. HARRIS

THE name Industrial Revolution probably brings to mind for most of us the Midlands and the North—factories, coal-fields, dreary towns, smoke and gloom; not the sunny holiday counties of the South-West. But the truth is that the extreme South-West was closely linked with the Revolution in its earlier days; it made its own distinct, indeed distinguished, contribution to the cumulative process in the later eighteenth and earlier nineteenth centuries by which great industries were built up on the new machines, the factory system, and the developed power of steam; all together turning Britain from a mainly agricultural nation into one that looked to manufacture and trade as its principal source of living.

It is a long story; but we can recall it briefly. In the sixteenth and seventeenth centuries the Cornish tinners had been drawn underground in the search for their "darling metal": in the eighteenth the market opened out for the copper that lay below the tin, and that drove them deeper still. But the deeper the mines the greater the problem of ridding them of water. The miners tried every device they knew to drain and pump, using man-power, horse-power, water-power. But they all had their limits; and Cornish mining might have been checked and stunted if some new power for pumping had not been brought to it.

The steam-engine saved it, and carried it on to the peaks of production through a hundred years. From the beginning of the eighteenth century a series of inventions brought steam-engines to a fair degree of efficiency. It was a West Countryman who produced the greatest. Thomas Newcomen, ironmonger of Dartmouth, built an engine which could be made by the smiths and carpenters and other craftsmen of the time, and could stand up to the hard wear and tear at the mines. Here, it seemed, was the power the miners wanted. But at once they met another limit: these Newcomen engines took enormous amounts of coal. Dr. Pryce, who wrote the standard book on Cornish mining, calls them "those devouring automatons". And every hundredweight of the coal had to be brought by sea, unloaded at the ports and carried on horse-back to the mines. This very traffic did much to develop the little port of Hayle, which gave an inlet to the western area. The Rev. Doctor Borlase, writing in the 1750's in his *Natural History of Cornwall*, says of it:

"'Tis a place of considerable trade for iron, Bristol wares, but more especially Welsh coal, for which at present there is such a demand for fire-engines, melting-houses, and the home consumption of a populous neighbourhood, that usually there are above five hundred, often times a thousand horses, which come to carry off coals . . . six days in the week. The fire-engines, which take off the greatest quantity of coal from this harbour, are still increasing in number. . . ."

The heavy costs involved in this transport might be prohibitive for the deeper mines. Clearly some new invention to cut the cost in full was the next need.

It was James Watt, of course, who solved the problem. In 1765 his invention (the separate condenser) gave equal power for one-third the coal or less. Ten years later his patent was extended to 1800. Then he joined forces with that prince among the manufacturers of his time, Matthew Boulton, to make one of the greatest partnerships in the history of British business. Boulton saw that they must find for the new engine a market where it could be developed, and flourish, and show the world its qualities; and that market was found in the mining industry of Cornwall. Soon the Cornish industrial adventurers were in touch with the partners, and orders were sent up. The chief item of the bargain made was that Boulton and Watt should be paid for the patent rights annual premiums equal to one-third the saving in fuel: it must have seemed a pretty good deal for the Cornishmen.

In August 1777 Watt travelled down to Cornwall to watch over the building of the first engines at Wheal Busy, the great mine at Chacewater, and at Ting Tang mine in Gwennap. Historically his mission was far more significant: he was forging a link between the early Industrial Revolution in the Midlands and the Cornish mining industry. His letters home to Boulton show how anxious he was, not to say a bit cross (he was much less assured than his partner). His opinions of local conditions and men were not by any means too flattering. The people, he says, "have the most ungracious manners of any people I was ever among"; the existing engines "are clumsy and nasty, the houses crackt and everything dripping with water". Later, under a lighter burden of worry, he made amendment.

It was not long before his engines proved an obvious success. In less than six years more than twenty had been set up, and soon it was reported that only one of the old type was still in action. That was the great conversion. The power for deep mining at reasonable cost had arrived, and Cornwall was the fertile ground for the early trials, so it was already playing its part in the great national revolution. It was not accomplished without struggle and dispute: very soon the differences came out. The premiums paid were heavy (Boulton and Watt did very well out of their Cornish business), and as years went on the saving in coal would not be so apparent. The adventurers complained and protested that they were paying too much, especially when in the 1780's the price of copper and tin fell. Then came depression: mine after mine fell out of the race of competition; unemployed miners revolted and demonstrated. In 1787 Mrs. Boscawen, writing the news of Cornwall to her friend, Mrs. Delany, speaks of " near a thousand angry miners marching into Truro to pull their houses about their ears ".

Still more serious than these troubles, from Boulton and Watt's point of view, were the rival inventions of engineers with ideas of their own. They brought out new forms of steam-engines which, they claimed, avoided Watt's patent rights. If they had made good these claims the premiums from the mines would have dried up. Of course the mine adventurers were keen on them! Boulton and Watt were furious, and bitter words were spoken and written. In the end the firm was vindicated at law. But in 1800 their patent ran out and with it the premiums; and to all intents they withdrew. That marked the end of the first period: it was in the next period that the greatest progress was made in the county.

The trouble with the inventors had been a sign of the times. Before Watt came there had been engineers in Cornwall working on the old engines. When his engines were ordered Watt sent down approved and highly skilled men, the chief and most trusted of them being William Murdoch, the young Scot. So around the mines grew quite a school of engineers, watching as each new engine was built, prompted again to improve upon performances. Invention was in the air: the school of engineers was a school of inventors; and out of it came two notable figures—William Murdoch himself and the younger Richard Trevithick. Murdoch helped Watt to improve the great engine. He also experimented on his own account, and produced a model locomotive, but only a model, no bigger than a good-sized toy. It must have been amusing to see him, like a huge boy, with the little engine, guiding it up and down the lanes around Redruth. But Watt did not agree: he wanted his workmen to concentrate on his schemes: he pooh-poohed the idea of "steam carriages" and he and Boulton dissuaded and coaxed Murdoch out of it. The same might have happened as disastrously (indeed for a time it did happen) to Murdoch's greatest invention, gas-lighting. In Redruth the house still stands where he worked out his first successful apparatus to light his own rooms. Beyond that he did not go till he had left Cornwall and gone back to Birmingham. He moves out of our story with his employers.

Murdoch was a man of stature among inventors. But the giant was the native Trevithick. He was a true child of the Revolution, brought up among the mines and engines. His very physique was a legend: men told for a generation how he threw the sledge-hammer over the roof of the engine-house. He was the same with high and low—genial, independent, forceful. Years later his faithful wife would tell how, when distinguished callers came to see the progress he was making with the engine, they were set to work there and then—Mr. Davies Giddy to be responsible for the stoking, Lady de Dunstanville to regulate the steam, no doubt under command. It is a revealing picture. One suspects that Trevithick measured the respectability of personages by their usefulness in promoting invention. It was a very proper standard for him to adopt: he was teaching men to use the drive of strong steam. His high-pressure engine packed power into a smaller compass: it could be built on to a carriage; and then the dream of the locomotive came true. In 1803 he ran his locomotive in the streets of London. But it remained a show-piece. He failed on the business side. He was more reckless than Watt; he could not be canny with money; and he never met his Matthew Boulton. In the end he died poor. But he had made his contribution. He had completed a cycle begun thirty years before. In the 1770's James Watt had brought his invention down to Cornwall to give new vigour to Cornish mining and engineering. Now, in the early nineteenth century, Trevithick had given back to the Industrial Revolution the high-pressure engine and the first locomotive. It was a handsome return. Lesser inventors added to the list. More and more various parts were made within the county, and the Cornish engine became a wonder of the engineering world. The

Cornish engineering industry that grew out of the Revolution earned then a distinction it has never lost.

There was science, too. Gentlemen scientists were often the companions of the engineers in experiment and invention—men like Robert Were Fox, the Quaker scientist of Falmouth; Davies Giddy, the scientific adviser of Trevithick; Humphry Davy, scientist and inventor in one. These were only the more famous figures in a remarkable growth of investigation, a growth that was firmly rooted in three societies that still exist —the Royal Geological Society of Cornwall, founded in 1814; the Royal Institution of Cornwall, in 1818; and the Royal Cornwall Polytechnic Society, in 1833. It was a renaissance of enterprise, and all classes seemed to be affected. The Cornish people were never more creative. The native industries, above all, mining, had developed their characteristics through the centuries, in all ranks, from the adventurer of means to the working miner who bargained for his pitch and worked it. Now the challenges of the new age brought them out vividly —the ready eye for sign of opportunity, the vision of great achievement and reward, the willingness to labour with furious energy and devoted skill.

The same qualities came out in quite different activities. These were times of excitement. We must remember that for nearly thirty of these years the country was at war with France, and enemy privateers might appear off the coast. Then, though there was prosperity, depression as surely followed; and hungry men were apt to riot. Above all, emotions flared out in the religious revivals that brought in wave after wave of Methodism. Sometimes they developed such power that they seemed to seize whole communities in their grip. For a century the Methodist movement ran parallel with the Industrial Revolution, strangely parallel in its phases. In 1743 John Wesley had followed his brother Charles to St. Ives, and over a period of nearly fifty years he made repeated visits to the county, to cultivate what was obviously a favourite field. Under his regulating hand societies grew and were ordered and guided; leaders were chosen, trained, and sent out to prove themselves by good report; and the Methodist movement in the far West became a strong constituent of the national connection. How the work had flourished, how Wesley himself and his Methodism had come to be accepted, followed, venerated, is summed up in the impressions of his last journey down. In his *Journal* he writes of Falmouth, "here, above forty years ago, I was taken prisoner by an immense mob, gaping and roaring like lions. But how is the tide turned! High and low now lined the street, from one end of the town to the other, out of stark love and kindness . . . staring as if the King were going by." The whole visit was a triumph, and as he left for the last time the old man was content to record, "so there is a fair prospect in Cornwall, from Launceston to the Land's End".

He was not mistaken. Under his influence and that

of the preachers that followed him thousands of the working classes flung away their old allegiances and habits, often, in their first zeal, their pleasures, their sports, their drinking, their adventures in smuggling (though that cost many a heart-searching!). They took, instead, to the disciplines Methodism demanded, built their bare chapels, and, what was more significant, the organizations in which new men came out and established a lead among their fellows. New men, new ways, new dominating organization: added up they amounted to a social revolution about men's homes as far-reaching as the technical revolution worked out among the mines. But here again it was inevitable, with the quickening of enterprise and the thrusts of a highly individualist society, that there should be differences and contention. After Wesley's death, when lesser men tried to impose narrower disciplines by rule, eager rebels broke away and formed new "connections" of their own. In the West, as elsewhere, the sects established themselves, particularly the Bible Christians, who sprang from the West Country peasantry and made a more direct emotional appeal to the lower working classes than the new Wesleyanism.

The impetus and fresh power brought to Cornish mining in the Industrial Revolution carried it forward through a hundred years, and for a time Cornwall was the leading producer in the world of tin and copper. But in the mid-nineteenth century new fields were developed abroad; prices fell while the deeper mines were becoming comparatively more costly at home; and the rich deposits of copper, on which so much of the prosperity was founded, dwindled. In the 1870's the industry slumped, and thousands of the mining people left the home districts that could no longer support them. They moved into other minefields in England or, more usually, took themselves overseas, east and west, to join the many hundreds of pioneers who had gone out before and carried with them the skills, the qualities, the ideas and the institutions that had come to be characteristic. At home the mining industry never fully recovered. For compensation in some measure there was the growth of the china clay industry and quarrying; engineering, which had begun as an aid to local mining, concentrated and adapted itself to world markets; and ship-repairing developed where Falmouth gave its magnificent harbour. So the scheme of industry changed to the pattern of the twentieth century, and one great span of history in the South-West, as in the whole nation, had been completed.

XVII

Victorian Provincial Life
by
JOHN BETJEMAN

THOUGH it is so near to us in time, the Victorian Age is so many miles from us in spirit and appearance that you will hardly recognize it. I hope you won't think I am sermonizing if I mention to you some general characteristics which apply to that age all over our land, and in particular in the West Country which, except in the coal district of Somerset and the mining area of Cornwall, was little touched by industrialism. I am not saying things were better, only that they were different—fundamentally different.

But to *see* Victorian West Country we must strip away much we now take for granted. We must rid the skyline of that clumsy collection of knitting-needles and string which takes the form of telephone and electric light poles with their wires, and ruins almost every village in the West.

Telegraph wires ran along railway lines, telephone

wires were unknown until late in the century. Roads were unmetalled, their hedges thick with dust in summer. Toll gates until 1878 were frequent; roadside towns like St. Columb, South Molton, Callington and Honiton, languished and longed for the railway as their inns decayed, their markets became less frequented and the silence in their streets grew deeper as custom left for shops in the towns which were lucky enough to have main-line railway stations.

Now in the sun-soaked silence of a summer morning, ninety years ago, let us walk down a village street. It looks like one of those coloured folding plates we used to find in that delightful West-Country publication, *Doidge's Annual*. Poultry are scratching in the dust of the road. The clink of the forge can be heard at the crossroads, and a cart-horse stands outside the smithy waiting to be shod. Huge lollipops, many of them home made, melt in bottles in the post-office window. The sweet smell of bread baking comes from an open cottage door. Thatch and cob walls in Devon, slate or granite walls and guttered slate roofs, all washed over white, predominate in Cornwall. The bright red ridge tiles from North Wales and the regular hard blue Welsh slates have as yet hardly appeared to outstare the old local roofs. Even by afternoon the village reprobate will be hopelessly drunk, for farmhouse cider is strong and so is home-made wine, and the beer at the inn has hops and malt in it. Few people have heard a train, much less seen one. The parish is the orbit of most people's lives, and a visit by farm-cart, gig or jingle, between high hedges, down steep hills where we all get out and walk, to cross by footbridge the stream at the bottom while the horse and cart splash through the ford—a visit to a town so small as South Molton or Callington is an adventure.

As for a trip to Exeter, Plymouth or Truro, that is an event which happens only two or three times in many a remote cottager's life, for these are capital cities, as distant-seeming, nay, more distant-seeming, than London is to-day. To go to London itself is like going to Brazil to-day, a rare distinction worthy of a lecture in the village on one's return. And, of course, there is the joke, time-honoured even then, about the farmer and his wife who thought all London was under glass since they went no farther than Paddington Station. Here and there are signs of the new middle class which rose in the Victorian Age. Old-fashioned farmers look askance at those younger farmers who are having their daughters taught to play the piano, and whose wives give tea-parties in parlours stuffed with gimcrack furniture, screens and painted fans and steel engravings. The old men think that a farm-woman's place is in the kitchen, and that farmer's daughters should learn cooking and preserving, instead of strumming Moore's *Melodies* on a new-fangled instrument.

But stay! Amid all this trim silence, what is the activity outside the parish church? Mr. St. Aubyn, the London architect, has just been here; the old box pews and the three-decker pulpit have been cut down at his command, and taken away for panelling or firewood; bright new pitch-pine pews replace them: the old, uneven roof has been tiled afresh and neatly guttered: the old stone walls have been repointed with cement so that they look quite new: the clear glass windows which buzzed with blue-bottles and gave a view of elmy slopes are to be filled with greenish glass which gives no view at all. The village instrumental choir has been disbanded and its old west gallery demolished.

Instead, we are to have a slap-up new chancel with an organ, and shiny tiles and stained-glass windows, a *cross* on the "Altar", and those old choir members who are not permanently offended or who are in mortal fear of the parson and squire (who are paying for these improvements) will be clothed in white samite, mystic, wonderful, and will "process" new from the vestry into their stalls. This is a time of religious controversy, fiercer and more full of hate even than modern politics. That great man, Henry Phillpotts, Bishop of Exeter, was an old-fashioned High Churchman. He ruled the diocese, which then included Cornwall, from 1830-69 with an iron rod. He was a loyal friend of the Church, courageous and uncompromising. No one could have called the see of Exeter the Dead See. In Phillpotts' reign, though the Church entrenched itself in the impregnable walls of doctrine, chapels sprung up like scarlet mushrooms at its feet. A glance at Kelly's Directory will show you how over Devon and Cornwall

the Free Churches, and particularly the Methodist followers of Wesley, built themselves preaching houses in
towns and villages during Phillpotts' reign. The church
for the squire and parson and their retainers, the chapel
for the smaller farmers and the merchants and tradesmen and poorer people. The division was often as
much social as theological, though we must not forget
that the doctrines of the Plymouth Brethren swept over
all ranks of Devon people in Queen Victoria's reign.

Let us step from such troubled waters, up the curv-
ing drive to the hall. Here there is every sign of prosperity. Gardeners clip the lawns around the house with
shears. The walled garden has acres of glass with a
vinery, an orchid house and a house for leaved plants
to be carried when at their stripiest and spottiest, to
decorate the entrance hall and drawing-room of the big
house. In winter there were coal fires in every bedroom.
Maidservants wear mob caps and scuttle away into cor-
ridors when anyone from the family approaches, for
servants are neither heard nor seen, except for the
butler and his hierarchy of footmen. And, of course,
the housekeeper and the lady's maid see their mistresses.
Sport is the occupation of most of the men. The
libraries of almost all country houses stop at about 1820,
and thereafter we find in them mostly sporting books.
Gun-rooms and billiard-rooms are built on to stately
houses; stables are enlarged; plate-glass windows, then
an expensive luxury, replaced the old leaded lights or
Georgian sash windows, giving the old houses a bombed

and hollow aspect. By the laws of primogeniture, eldest sons only inherited the house and estate, younger sons went into the services—in Devon and Cornwall it was as often the Navy as the Army—and into the Church. The son who went into the Church usually inherited the family living. The Rev. S. Baring-Gould of Lew Trenchard was a Devon squarson in this tradition. But these laws of inheritance had their unwritten laws of obligation. Poor relations of the family paid annual visits to the house and stayed sometimes for weeks. They were welcomed and expected. There is no question that a village with a rich and benevolent landowner living in its big house was a more compact and law-abiding unit than some remoter hamlets given over to magic, cruelty, drunkenness and small farmers—of which we may read in Hawker's letters and essays and Fortescue's books. It is also hard to believe that a public institution or a government office in a country house is so friendly and personal a neighbour as a landowner.

And except on these estates where absentee landlords left their affairs in the hands of a grasping, pitiless agent, the farm-workers, gardeners, game-keepers and small farmers of the Victorian period were kindly treated. Each village was like a family with the squire as father and his wife as mother, the latter with her daughters bringing round soup and jellies to cottagers who were ill, the farmer with his sons as keen on sport (except, of course, poaching) as his tenants, and providing work for the men. Of course this feudal family, like all big families, had its rebels among the children. But read any stories or novels of the Victorian West Country—Henry Kingsley, Charlotte M. Yonge, Hardy, Eden Phillpotts, "Q", Baring-Gould, Fortescue—and you will find that those words of Hymn 537, *Ancient and Modern*:

> *The rich man in his castle,*
> *The poor man at his gate,*
> *He made them high and lowly,*
> *And ordered their estate,*

—that those words expressed what was generally accepted. It occurred to few to question the settled social order. The squire was still temporal lord of the village, just as the parson was spiritual lord.

Victorian towns of Devon and Cornwall I have left till last, because when one thinks of the West one thinks of country first and town second.

Seaside resorts were a Georgian creation. Sidmouth, Teignmouth and Torquay still have neat, stucco villas of the late Georgian age with wide verandas, broad eaves and an ilex tree on the lawn. And, of course, Devon had long been popular for holidays—Torquay, for example, with its palms, myrtles and blue sea, and its Italianate buildings—because Torquay was thought to resemble Italy.

But in Victoria's reign these modest places were transformed out of recognition. And the transformation, of course, was brought about by the railways. In the fifties railways had reached Plymouth from London via Bristol and Exeter. In '59 Brunel's great bridge across the Tamar at Saltash was finished, and Cornwall was connected with England by steam. The London & South-Western soon came hurrying down to Exeter from Waterloo by a shorter though more difficult route, and filled in the gaps in North Devon and North Cornwall left by the Great Western, buying up local lines and opening branch railways with gay abandon.

From the sixties onwards seaside places flourished. Then the rows of lodging-houses appeared all the way from the station to the front, then the Gothic suburban churches were built from designs by R. Medley Fulford, then the circulating libraries did a roaring trade in the season and shell boxes appeared at the fancy goods shops and piers jutted out into the water and local marbles were worked up into souvenirs, and bathing-machines lined the shore.

Later a more sophisticated taste, inspired by the Morris movement and a love of the simple life, turned from these seaside resorts and left them to the vulgar and to retired Colonial officials, and found solace instead in fishermen's coves in quaint nooks and uneven cobbles and smelly lobster pots and rugged fishermen of Cornwall. By the end of the century, St. Ives, Polperro and Looe, Boscastle and Clovelly drew the artistic and discriminating who sketched, etched and painted the scenes we know so well, finding in Cornwall and North Devon a second Brittany.

As for Exeter, Plymouth and Truro, they ceased to be the capitals they had been, and became provincial towns. County families gave up their town houses and bought houses in the newly built squares of London or, hit by agricultural depression, gave up having a town house at all. Though county families withdrew, hotels and suburbs increased; the old square-paned Georgian shops were supplanted by acres of plate-glass window: big drapers opened (often owned by Welshmen), overhead miniature railways carrying change whizzed in and out of pennants of Nottingham lace and lengths of silk and satin. The beautiful broad Union Street between Plymouth and Devonport was no longer broad, for greedy commerce ordained that the front gardens of its houses should be covered with shops. Similar spoliation may be seen in the streets of most other towns. We stood so high in the world's esteem, our trade was so thriving, our industrial North was hammering away so late into the night, that our shops were stocked with wonderful things, competition was vigorous, visitors increased and so did the town's population (generally at the expense of the small market towns without railways or only with branch lines). In Plymouth, Exeter, Truro and Redruth, everything seemed to be getting better and better. Then it was that people seriously thought bigger was better and more was merrier and a material paradise on earth was approach-

ing. Mayors glowed in their chairs. Municipal enterprise increased. Streets were lighted with gas lamps.
Town halls were built bigger than the biggest churches
—like Norman and Hine's now-bombed Guildhall at
Plymouth (1870). Enormous cemeteries were opened
on hill slopes, new spires pricked the skyline of hills
serrated with suburbs. Elementary schools rose out of
asphalt playgrounds.

Merchants and councillors were men of consequence
and lived in large villas on the outskirts of the towns,
with an entrance drive in front and coach-houses at
the back. Public libraries, institutes and reading-rooms
disseminated culture. Electric tramways spread the
towns out into the country. But never was the West
Country so badly hit by what was then called "progress" as most other parts of England. Still the country
remained, and agriculture and fishing held their own.
Still county differences survived.

Thus it is that Devon and Cornwall, Dorset, Somerset
and Wilts still remain like another country within our
island as yet not quite suburbanized, not quite given
over to the chain store and the farming syndicate, the
local government official and his ally in Whitehall. The
sins of the Victorians in the West were of a gentler
kind than in the North and in the Midlands; though
they ruined many old churches with their "restora-
tions", spoiled many old high streets and sprinkled the
outskirts of towns with more mean houses than magnificent ones, it was not the Victorian but our own age

which ruined the wild West Coast with bungalows and strung the sky with wires, littered the roadsides with shacks and hoardings, turned old inns into glittering pretension and floodlit the whole with fluorescent light —all in the name of the god of "progress" whom the Victorians invented.

XVIII

The West in English History
by
A. L. ROWSE

I HOPE that this series has brought home to you, if nothing else, the extraordinary richness and diversity of the contribution the West has made to English history and the life of the country in general. You know —each English county is a world in itself; and it is really true, though you may not at first credit it, that it takes a life-time to know a single county properly. That is to say, if you are going to know all its parishes and churches and towns, the farms and fields, the earth-works, camps, rivers and bridges, the houses with all their pictures and memories and associations, the people who have lived in them, the books and letters they wrote, the monuments and documents of all those vanished lives that were once as active as we and have the interest for us that they were our ancestors: they gave us life; they made and handed down these things.

There is the fascination of inhabiting an old, rich,

storied soil like ours; personally I could not bear to inhabit a new and raw one. Whatever else may be taken from us, these riches remain—if we treasure them.

But the very richness of these things makes it all the more difficult for me to sum up the character of the West and its place in the English story—there is so much diversity. And yet we all can recognize that the West has a certain common character. The difficulty is to define it—to put salt on the tail of that particular shy bird. Perhaps we can think of it best like a railway journey home to the West—like the journey home to Cornwall that I make from Oxford at the end of every term, the railway stringing these familiar, much-loved counties along its thread. (I hasten to add that in addition to the usual route through Berks, Wilts, Somerset, Devon, I have gone home by the southern route, via Hants and Dorset, Winchester and Salisbury, as well as from Gloucester and Bristol: all the various routes, in fact, by which the Saxons invaded the ancient kingdom of Dumnonia.) You may think of it as the reverse of the wonderful march of the Cornish army up through the country in the Civil War.

Dr. Hoskins has given us a clue: you notice as you go westward the landscape changes: it becomes more varied and yet more intimate, it becomes so much older, more storied, with longer memories of the past. It is less man-made, or at any rate less recently man-made: it appeals to instincts so deep in us that we are not con-

scious of them. I believe that in that lies something of
the secret of the extraordinary magnetic hold it has
over us—to a degree hardly explicable. Everybody
instinctively wants to go West—as if the golden Hes-
perides are there and nowhere else. You never hear
of anybody wanting to go East—not in that same deep,
primeval sense.

A Suffolk man I know who had got his heart's desire
—a famous fragment of an old great house in Cornwall—once told me that he hoped never to cross the
Tamar again. He was quite a young man and other-
wise quite normal. It is extraordinary, but everybody
feels the draw of the West.

Like the landscape, the West in a general sense has
always been more conservative, more tenacious of old
cultures and associations, old ways and habits. The
layers there are thicker and less disturbed, and that
gives greater character and individuality—not neces-
sarily more pleasant, I hasten to add; but it is something to have character and individuality in a world
that has progressively less of them. The West has been
socially and culturally more conservative; and yet in
recent centuries it has shown strong strains and traditions of Radicalism. For example in the Puritan
peasantry and small clothing towns of Dorset and
Somerset and East Devon, that took part in Monmouth's Rebellion and shifted into Nonconformity,
which became very strong in the West Country,
stronger as you go farther west, until in Cornwall it

numbered the majority. Politically that meant that in modern times the West has had a strong Liberal and even Radical tradition. For if it was true as Disraeli said that the Church of England was the Conservative Party at prayer, it was almost equally true that Nonconformity was the Liberal Party at prayer. I think all that springs from the *Individualism* that I find a leading characteristic of the West—and individualism which also gets stronger the farther west you go, until it becomes too much of a good thing with the Cornish. But then they *are* different: there never was such a joke as the Cornish motto, "One and All": heaven knows where they got it from: it must be very recent.

All the same, the individualism of the West is a good thing, especially in a world that is becoming all too uniform and standardized. And that individualism is very deep-rooted: it springs out of the ultimate structure of society in the West, the scattered farmsteads and hamlets, about which Dr. Hoskins writes with such historical imagination and penetrative understanding. "Chalk is Chapel and Cheese is Church", so goes the saying; and these things tie up together, the culture of a people, their religion and their politics, with the very lie of the landscape.

I have always thought it symptomatic that in politics the extreme West should have produced a rather harsh and unattractive type of doctrinaire: Sir John Eliot, for example, Sir William Molesworth and Lord Courtney, Aclands and Foots: I used to notice the same

symptoms in myself, until I turned over a new leaf—
or rather, turned over a whole public library.   (But
perhaps the old Adam is still there waiting to catch
me!)

As for the contribution of the West to our history,
what are we to say?

I think we can say that there are three points at which
it has had a decisive effect.

First, Alfred and Wessex saved England for the English from the Danes.   Wessex became the foundation
stone of the kingdom.   There is a certain charm in the
thought that the Dorset dialect of William Barnes is
the lineal descendant of the English spoken at the
court of King Alfred.   And what a stroke of imagination it was on Thomas Hardy's part to call into existence once more, after a thousand years, the ancient
kingdom of Wessex and people it with the living crea-
tions of his mind.

Second, there has been the extraordinary influence of
the western seamen in our history.

What made the fortunes of England as a country in
the modern era was the discovery of America.   In all
that oceanic movement which made the greatness of
our country—turned us from being a small people on
the edge of the known world into the foremost and most
dynamic people in modern history—the lead was taken
by the western seamen.   As Dr. Williamson shows us,
Atlantic enterprise began from Bristol, with those
pioneer voyages set on foot by the Bristol merchants,

culminating in the discovery of North America, by Cabot. After that followed the enterprises of the Hawkinses from Plymouth in Africa, South America, the West Indies; Drake's voyage round the world; the colonizing ventures of Gilbert, Raleigh, Grenville, the *Mayflower*, Sir Ferdinando Gorges, John White of Dorchester, John Pym and innumerable others, from whose efforts the Empire and the English-speaking world took shape. The fact that North America is inhabited by English-speaking stocks is the decisive fact, thank goodness, in the modern world. We owe that very largely to the original enterprise, daring and imagination of western folk, seamen, colonists, empire-builders. (It was quite right that Richard Hakluyt, who helped to plan it and wrote it up in his great book, *The Principal Navigations*, should have held a stall in Bristol cathedral: Bristol, capital and inspiration of the West, with all its crowding memories, still though sorely wounded by enemy and barbarian alike, still one of the most beautiful of the great cities of England.)

Third, there is the remarkable part played by Cornwall in the early stages of the Industrial Revolution: the development of the steam-engine, the technical achievements in mining which led to Cornish miners and engineers taking such a lead in opening up mines all over the world, in North and South America, in Australia and South Africa and, latest of all, Malaya. All that is a very striking and distinctive achievement. There is a most wonderful story to be written, that of the Cornish emigration all over the world—even more wonderful than the comings and goings among the Celtic people in the Age of the Saints, which have left such a mark in our place-names. What a book that would make—if only someone had the enterprise and imagination to write it.

As for the separate contributions of the western counties to that creative amalgam that is England, I cannot do justice to the theme—it would need a series of broadcasts to itself. Now I can only give a few hints for you to follow up. Here, too, Dr. Hoskins has given us a clue: the number of great families, of great men, that have sprung up from those little Western homesteads: Tremaynes, Boscawens, Edgcumbes, Raleighs, Gilberts, Drakes, Hoods, Hardys. Only the other day in the remote parish of St. Clether I stood and looked over the gate into the little farm place of Treraven, where the great Admiral Hawke was born and brought up as a boy. I thought of his feelings when he first left home for Plymouth to join his ship—and all that great career at sea, including one of the most splendid of victories, Quiberon Bay. Or there is that charming, hardly changed Elizabethan farm-house, up the lane from East Budleigh church, where Walter Raleigh was born: there, too, just over the brow of the hill, you can see the sea.

Though a Cornishman myself, I think of Devon as the heart of the West Country, and Exeter as its historic centre from Roman times to this. And really the contribution of Devon men to the genius and achievement of the country has been prodigious; though Wiltshire comes very near to it with some among the greatest—Clarendon among statesmen and historians, Hobbes among philosophers, Sir Thomas Lawrence among painters, and among architects Sir Christopher Wren.

Yet Somerset produces an equally first-class team: to set against Hobbes, John Locke; against Clarendon, John Pym; and what about Dunstan, greatest of Anglo-Saxon statesman-bishops; Henry Fielding among novelists; Robert Blake and Sam Hood among sailors? Nevertheless the strongest contingent of seamen of any English county, north or south, east or west, comes from Devon and it is captained by Drake, the "fortunate captain" of his age. Next runner-up comes Cornwall with a very strong team: Hawke and Boscawen, Grenville, Lord Exmouth, Bligh of the *Bounty*. What is less generally realized is Devonshire's extraordinary record in the matter of painters. We all recognize East Anglia's ascendancy; but county for county Devon runs Norfolk and Suffolk very close with two of the greatest of English painters, Reynolds and Turner, with Nicholas Hilliard, most brilliant of Elizabethan miniaturists, with Hudson and Northcote, Samuel Prout, and Francis Towne. There is not much point in merely mentioning great writers like the Elizabethan Richard Hooker, or the poet Coleridge, or the historian Froude; there are whole families in which genius ran, in the Coleridges, the Kingsleys, the Froudes. I must draw your attention rather to one who influenced the whole history of Europe: St. Boniface of Crediton, who not only missionized and converted large sections of the Germans to Christianity, but reorganized the Frankish Church: one of the greatest Englishmen who ever lived. And lastly the lawyer Bracton, to whom our medieval law largely owed its shape: you will see where he lies now, just in front of the rood-screen in Exeter cathedral. What a company it is for any county!—but I am not making a list: there would be no end to it.

I have only chosen Devon as a central example. One could do almost the same for any of the western counties—Cornwall would come out rather remarkably considering that it laboured under the disadvantage of speaking Cornish for so many centuries. The truth is that the soil of this island is rich beyond belief in the things of the mind—worth more than all the dollars of America. Treasure them—they will never fail you; explore them—there is no end to their interest. And in the course of it you will yourself become more interesting and all the happier for fulfilling your own potentialities of mind and spirit.

to the Coleridges, the Kingsleys, the Froudes. I must draw your attention rather to one who influenced the whole history of Europe: St. Boniface of Crediton; who not only missionized and converted large sections of the Germans to Christianity, but reorganized the Frankish Church, one of the greatest Englishmen who ever lived; and lastly the lawyer Bracton, to whom our mediæval law largely owed its shape; you will see where he lies now, just in front of the rood-screen in Exeter cathedral. What a company it is for any county!—but I am not making a list; there would be no end to it.

I have only chosen Devon as a central example. One could do almost the same for any of the western counties—Cornwall would come out rather remarkably considering that it laboured under the disadvantage of speaking Cornish for so many centuries. The truth is that the soil of this island is rich beyond belief in the things of the mind—worth more than all the dollars in America. Treasure them—they will never fail you; exploit them—there is no end to their interest. And in the course of it you will yourself become more interesting and all the happier for fulfilling your own potentialities of mind and spirit.

List of Books

Readers may find the following list of books useful. It is hoped that it will provide sufficient material for the study of the various periods of English and regional history covered in these talks. So far from being exhaustive it is merely a practical beginning.

1. GENERAL HISTORIES

History of England: G. M. Trevelyan (Longmans)
English Social History: G. M. Trevelyan (Longmans)
The Evolution of England: J. A. Williamson (O.U.P.)
The Spirit of English History: A. L. Rowse (Cape)

2. BOOKS ABOUT THE SUBJECT OF THESE TALKS

(These are arranged in the same order as the talks)

Roman Britain: R. G. Collingwood (O.U.P.)
Roman Britain: Ian Richmond ("Britain in Pictures" series—Collins)
The Life and Times of Alfred the Great: C. Plummer (O.U.P.)
Origins of the West Saxon Kingdom: G. M. Young (O.U.P.)

187

The Archaeology of Cornwall and Scilly: H. O'N. Hencken (Methuen)

William the Conqueror: Sir F. M. Stenton (Putnam)

The Medieval Village: G. G. Coulton (C.U.P.)

The Monastic Order in England: M. D. Knowles (C.U.P.)

Somerset Historical Essays, 1921: J. Armitage Robinson (O.U.P.)

The Times of St. Dunstan: J. Armitage Robinson (O.U.P.)

The English Medieval Wool Trade: Eileen Power (O.U.P.)

Cornish Essays: Charles Henderson (O.U.P.)

Devonshire Scenery: ed. Rev. Wm. Everitt (Wm. Pollard, Exeter)

Cornwall and the Cornish: A. K. Hamilton Jenkin (Dent)

Tudor Cornwall: A. L. Rowse (Cape)

The Ocean in English History: J. A. Williamson (O.U.P.)

The Voyages of the Cabots: J. A. Williamson (Argonaut Press)

Sir Richard Grenville: A. L. Rowse (Cape)

Sir John Hawkins: J. A. Williamson (O.U.P.)

Cornwall in the Great Civil War: M. Coate (O.U.P.)

History of the Rebellion: Clarendon, ed. Macray (O.U.P.)

History of the Great Civil War: S. R. Gardiner (Longmans)

The Civil War in Dorset: A. R. Bayley (Barnicott and Pearce)

From Trackway to Turnpike: Gilbert Sheldon (O.U.P.)

Travels Through England on a Side-Saddle: Celia Fiennes (Cresset Press)

Tour Through England and Wales: Daniel Defoe (Everyman)

Monmouth: E. D. D'Oyley (Bles, 1938)

The Trial of the Bloody Assizes: ed. J. G. Muddiman (Hodge, Edinburgh)

The Wiltshire Woollen Industry: G. D. Ramsay (O.U.P.)

...e Gateway of Empire: C. M. Macinnes (Arrowsmith)
...ath: Brian Little (Batsford)
...ath: R. A. L. Smith (Batsford)
...ife and Letters at Bath in the Eighteenth Century: A. Barbeau (Heinemann)
Rural Rides: William Cobbett (Everyman)
The Cornish Miner: A. K. Hamilton Jenkin (Dent)
Richard Trevithick, Engineer and Man: Dickinson and Titley (C.U.P.)
Development of Transportation in Modern England: W. T. Jackman (C.U.P.)
Portrait of an Age: G. M. Young (O.U.P.)
My Native Devon: John Fortescue (Macmillan)
The Life and Letters of R. S. Hawker: C. E. Byles (Bodley Head)
Cornwall: Claude Berry (Hale)

3. LOCAL HISTORIES

These books were written by the local historians and antiquaries. They contain much fascinating reading, but they can for the most part only be obtained from libraries. A convenient series of more modern county histories is that published by Elliot Stock in the nineteenth century. For Bristol, Winchester, and Exeter consult also the "Historic Towns" series (Longmans).

Gloucestershire: Sir R. Atkins
Survey of Cornwall: R. Carew
Somerset: J. Collinson
Wiltshire: Sir R. Colt Hoare
Dorset: J. Hutchins
Worthies of Devon: J. Prince

The West in English History